# *Mosaics*
## Piece by Piece

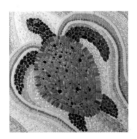

David and Charles

# FOREWORD

David & Charles is an F+W Publications Inc. company
4700 East Galbraith Road
Cincinnati, OH 45236s

First published in the UK in 2007

A catalogue record for this book is available from the British
Library.

ISBN-13: 978-0-7153-2766-1 paperback
ISBN-10: 0-7153-2766-6 paperback

Printed in China by SNP Leefung
for David & Charles
Brunel House    Newton Abbot    Devon

Visit our website at www.davidandcharles.co.uk

David & Charles books are available from all good bookshops;
alternatively you can contact our Orderline on 0870 9908222 or
write to us at FREEPOST EX2 110, D&C Direct, Newton Abbot, TQ12
4ZZ (no stamp required UK only); US customers call 800
289-0963 and Canadian customers call 800-840-5220.

**Concept and editing:** Monique Rahner
**Layout - contents:** Heike Wenger
**Photos:** frechverlag GmbH, 70499 Stuttgart; Fotostudio Ullrich &
Co., Renningen
**Pieces:** Bruno Rodi (page 35 [house number], 37 bottom, 46, 47
bottom, 52 bottom, 53 top, 61, 70/71, 72 right, 78, 90/91, 101, 103,
107, 108/109, 110/111, 112, 119, 120/121 and 123), Catherine Massey
(page 36, 47 top, 53 bottom, 59, 63, 65, 72 left, 73, 75, 77, 81, 85, 89,
93, 95, 98/99, 115, 117 and 125) and Lea Ciambelli (page 37 top, 52
top, 56, 67, 68/69, 82/83, 87, 97 and 105)

Welcome to *Mosaics Piece by Piece*, where you can learn about the
ancient art of creating mosaics. Step-by-step instructions show you
what to do, in the same way as you would make a mosaic stone by
stone. After a brief introduction to the main mosaic materials, you wi
learn what to consider when creating your design, as well as how the
colours selected, direction of flow and colour of the grout can affect
the mosaic.

The subsequent practical sections demonstrate the advantages and
disadvantages of both the direct and indirect mosaic methods, that is,
directly placing the tesserae onto the base or working on a temporary
surface first, such as paper. There is also a whole section devoted to
making mosaic objects.

After each practical section, you will find projects ideas for your own
mosaic work, so that you can start practising what you have learned in
the workshop.

Once you have completed the workshop, you can reap the rewards of
your labours by moving on to the main projects section. This is a collection of large and small mosaics for the home and garden. There are
simple pieces for beginners, as well as more demanding pieces for
those experienced with mosaics.

We hope you have fun learning about mosaic techniques and wish you
every success with producing your own creations!

Your team of experts

# CONTENTS

# 1
## MATERIALS

# 2
## DESIGNING
## MOSAICS

# 3
## TOOLS AND
## EQUIPMENT

# 4
## DIRECT
## METHOD

# 5
## INDIRECT
## METHOD

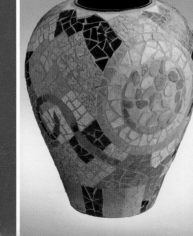

# 6
## MOSAIC
## OBJECTS

# WORKSHOP

## Step-by-step approach

Whether you are interested in the direct or indirect method of laying mosaics, you will learn exactly what to do step by step in the workshop. Following a brief introduction to the various mosaic tesserae, possible bases, adhesives and grouts, the two main ways of making mosaics will be explained to you in detail: directly sticking onto the object or working indirectly onto a temporary surface. You will also be introduced to working with supports, such as netting, as well as reciprocal laying and the flat cast. There is also an extra section on the subtleties of working with three-dimensional objects.

## Projects to excite you

The practical workshop sections are accompanied by projects. The examples given will enable you to practise what you have just learned. You will only require the knowledge you have gained so far. So, in the projects for direct laying, you will find simple pieces on which you can practise your knowledge of designing the surface area and, in particular, sticking on the mosaic stones using the correct grout. With the indirect method, you will practise creating completely flat surfaces.

## Templates for quick copying

Some people are simply inspired by the colourful world of images around them, whereas others prefer to copy motifs exactly. To make this quick and easy, you will find all the necessary templates from page 126 onwards in this book. They have been reduced in size and can be enlarged to their original size using the suggested enlargement percentage. On page 13, you will also learn how you can enlarge the templates by hand using the grid supplied.

## Advice

◆ It takes practice to make a mosaic. Start off with small ones, with simple patterns, made from a manageable amount of tesserae in geometric shapes (square, rectangle, triangle or trapezium), or by using nuggets or pebbles, for example. It's really important at the outset that you get lots of practice in sticking the tesserae in place. When you begin to get a feel for working with mosaics, you can tackle larger pieces and more detailed cutting.

◆ When in the process of cutting tesserae and working with cement-based powders (tiling adhesive and grout), remember to wear protective clothing – safety goggles, gloves and dust mask.

# 1 MATERIALS

## Advice

◆ All over Europe you will find magnificent examples of mosaic art, for example, in the churches of Ravenna, Italy, on buildings by Antonio Gaudí and Lluis Domènech i Montaner in Barcelona, Spain, as well as on sculptures by Niki de Saint Phalle in the famous Tarot garden in Tuscany, Italy. Artistic ornamentation can also be studied in the Islamic world, such as on mosques in Dubai or Jerusalem, or as part of Moorish architecture in Morocco.

Mosaics are made by placing tiny pieces of a particular material together and sticking them firmly to the backing surface. The pictures are often of people or are ornamental in nature. The word 'mosaic' probably comes from Greek and means 'dedicated to the muses'. The materials used most frequently are glass, ceramic and natural stone, yet pebbles, shells and other found objects also work well. The tesserae (the term for mosaic materials) are fitted together on flat or raised surfaces. Initially, mosaics were used exclusively as coverings for floors, which meant that the materials had to meet functional requirements. Later, when walls were also used, small pieces of glass and then ceramic were employed, as well as pebbles and natural stone. Today, the only limitation on materials that can be used is the subsequent intended use of the item. So why not experiment with materials that you like and can easily get hold of?

Natural stone – requires some practise to use

Ceramic – wide selection and available cheaply

Glass mosaics – industrially made and available in many colours

Found and collected obj[ects], anything is possible

# GLASS TESSERAE

### Glass stones (industrial mosaic)

These little stones are also called industrial mosaic. They are made from glass that is coloured by adding metal oxides, which makes it opaque.

The stones are available in 1cm (⅜in) and 2cm (¾in) squares. Their flat upper surface (the underside is grooved) and their even thickness, about 4mm (⅛in) makes them easy to cut using a glass cutter or glass nibbling pincers (see page 21).

Industrial mosaic is resistant to moisture and frost, and holds its colour for a long time, even when subjected to the elements. There is a large colour palette to choose from, especially in the green and blue shades, where a wide selection is available. The stones are available loose, as well as stuck to 32cm² (12½in²) sheets of paper or netting (pull them off the netting or remove the paper by soaking in water).

## Broken glass and mirrored glass

When making mosaic objects, interesting effects can be achieved with broken glass from cars. You can obtain this for free from breaker's yards. Many mosaic material suppliers also sell satinized or mirrored varieties, known as ice glass.

As well as broken glass from cars, shards of mirror are also good for mosaic work. You can often get these free of charge from glaziers. Look for pieces that are of the same thickness, which will make them easier to work with. Due to its homogenous structure, mirrored glass is easy to cut with a glass cutter and breaking pincers (see pages 21 and 24), even for beginners. Always score first on the top.

### Advice

◆ The traditional glass or natural stone cubes were known as tesserae (singular tessera). Nowadays, the term is used for pieces of any type of material in various shapes, such as irregular pieces of broken tile, industrially made glass or ceramic stones, all kinds of found objects, shells or pebbles.

◆ Industrial mosaic is also available in a marble effect and threaded with gold.

◆ As well as industrial glass, molten glass slabs are available – a primary product of the manufactue of Venetian smalti (see page 8). They are opaque and 1cm (⅜in) thick.

◆ Tiffany glass is used to make lanterns and other transparent mosaic objects. This is 3mm (⅛in) thick and available from artisan glaziers. Small, leftover pieces can be bought very cheaply.

Glass tesserae continued

Glass tesserae
continued

## Smalti

Smalti is enamelled Venetian glass: the classic mosaic material. It is still painstakingly made by hand today: the molten glass is coloured and poured into a glass mould, a flat disc about 20cm (8in) in diameter. It is then broken into individual stones about 1.5 x 1cm (⅝ x ⅜in), 7mm (just over ¼in) thick. The upper surface of Smalti is uneven, which means that they are mainly used for decoration and not for flat surfaces. The upper surface is also partially pitted with air bubbles, which is why a mosaic made from smalti is often left ungrouted, since the grout collects in the holes and spoils the intense colour of the stones. Smalti come in a very wide range of colours and reflect the light effectively, producing a light sparkle, due to their uneven upper surface. The stones are made in a traditional way using a mosaic hammer and awl or broken using mosaic nippers. They are available from various Italian suppliers (in Murano).

## Advice

◆ Smalti are extremely expensive, which is why they are not suitable for beginners.

## Tips & Tricks

◆ Imitation gold and silver stones can be obtained cheaply for decorative work. Paint acrylic paint over the back of a transparent glass slab. Otherwise, use silicone adhesive to stick metal foil from a craft shop to the glass.

## Gold and silver stones

Gold tesserae were historically mainly used in Byzantine art to form the background. The stones consist of thin yellow or white gold leaf embedded between two layers of glass for stability and also to protect the precious inset layer. The lower piece of glass is often dyed. Transparent glass stones can be used on both sides. The tesserae come in different square shapes 1cm (⅜in), 2cm (¾in) and 5cm (2in) edge lengths) and are available in a thickness of 4.5–4.7mm (about ³⁄₁₆in). As well as stones with flat surfaces, there are also stones with irregular, rippled surfaces. The tesserae are made by hand in Italy (also in other metallic colours) and are very expensive.

# CERAMIC TESSERAE

## Glazed ceramic (stoneware)

Stoneware is mainly used to make tiles for interiors. The fragment is white or red (the colour has no bearing on the quality) and is covered in a thin, coloured glaze. Stoneware, available in a variety of shapes and sizes, is easy to shape with glass and tile cutters, as well as a hammer or mosaic nippers. The colour palette usually depends on bathroom fashions. Large tile producers often offer a long-term selection of single-coloured tiles. Stoneware is not really suitable for the indirect (or reverse) method (see page 38 onwards), since the colour of the reverse side does not correspond to the top. Another limitation of stoneware is that it is not always frost-resistant.

Irregular-shaped pieces can now be obtained too (see photo above right), with a glazed broken edge (the glaze is applied after firing).

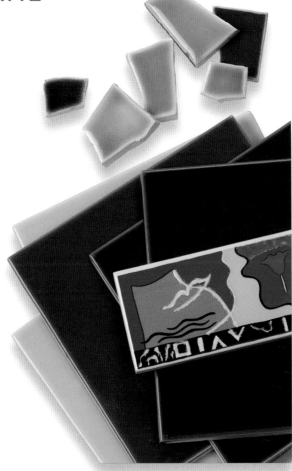

## Tips & Tricks

◆ Highly fired floor tiles are more difficult to cut than low-fired wall tiles.

◆ Glazed ceramic is available in a variety of different thicknesses, which makes it very difficult to achieve a level surface using the direct technique with leftover pieces. So, if you want to make, for example, a dining plate, it is best to use the reciprocal technique (see page 42).

◆ Mini and macro ceramic tesserae are special tiles between just 3mm (1/8in) and 5mm (3/16in) in size, which are good for jewellery or emblems (that is, small inlaid mosaic work).

## Crockery fragments

Whether it's a current crockery design from the sales in a department store or a rarity from the past found in a flea market, working with these fragments requires a great deal of collecting of the basic material. A hammer and mosaic nippers are good for this task. The smaller the individual pieces, the slighter their curvature and the flatter the surface of the mosaic.

## Advice

◆ Glass nibbling pincers are not suitable for working with ceramic stoneware.

◆ Other rocks can also be used for mosaic work. Alabaster, for example, comes in white, pink, grey, a browny shade and sometimes black. It is fairly soft and so is good to work with, but it is not very weather-resistant. Sandstone and travertine are also both good to work with, although sandstone crumbles easily.

## Tips & Tricks

◆ A wide variety of natural stones are commercially available. Sometimes you can also arrange to have strips cut, but only at a stonemason's.

◆ Ready-made, cut natural stone tesserae all come in the same thickness. This saves having a deep bed of mortar when laying them, which would otherwise even out the varied thicknesses of the materials. At the same time, you get a very level surface.

## Unglazed ceramic (stoneware)

Unglazed ceramic stoneware comes in the form of very highly fired, ready-made ceramic tiles with an edge length of 2cm (¾in) or 2.3cm (¹⁵⁄₁₆in) and a thickness of 4mm (⁵⁄₃₂in). Unglazed ceramic stoneware is moisture- and frost-resistant, and can easily be cut with a glass cutter and breaking pincers (for exact geometric shapes) or with tile nippers (see pages 21 and 22). The stones have sharp, right-angled corners, are unglazed and are evenly coloured. They are mainly available in earthy, muted shades. They are the cheapest of the ready-made stones and are very good for reproducing ancient mosaic pictures, which were originally made from marble.

# NATURAL STONE TESSERAE

## Limestone and marble

Any natural stone can be used for mosaics. However, if you have ever tried to split a piece of granite, you will know the limitations. Also, materials with pronounced layering, such as slate, are very difficult to split. In contrast, most types of marble and limestone are good. Natural stones are available ready-cut, for example, cubes with a 1cm (⅜in) edge length. These stones are usually cut from slabs of uniform thickness, have a flat surface and slightly rounded edges. Stones with an edge length of 1cm (⅜in) with two broken and four cut sides are available. When creating mosaics, the broken side should be uppermost.

You can make tiles yourself from strips of stone (have them cut by a stonemason) that can be split using a mosaic hammer and awl (see page 26).

The colour palette for limestone ranges from white, through a yellowy shade to light grey. Darker shades appear due to pollution. Marble is harder than limestone and is available in different colours from white, through green, yellow and brown to black.

# FOUND OBJECTS

## Shells and pebbles

Shells and pebbles are both highly decorative and suitable for mosaic work where a level surface is irrelevant. Pebbles can be found in all sorts of colours, other than blue/grey, such as yellow, green and reddish brown. Working with pebbles involves a lot of collecting in advance. It is virtually impossible to use the indirect (or reverse) method (see page 38 onwards), as a smooth surface is difficult to obtain.

## Tips & Tricks

◆ Thin muscle shells should be filled with tile adhesive before being glued, otherwise the adhesive surface will be too limited and the risk of breakage too high.

◆ If your plan is to incorporate metal or other buttons with loops on the reverse into your mosaic, the loops must be removed before gluing. Cutting pliers or pincers are good for this task.

## Glass nuggets, buttons and other materials

Many other materials can be used to produce mosaics: glass nuggets are available in many different shapes (such as half-spheres, hearts or fish) and sizes from craft shops or suppliers, or the relevant sections in department stores. They can have a transparent, shimmering or satinized surface. Pretty buttons, pearls, fragments of glass, clay or terracotta decorations, metal shapes and many other items can be effectively incorporated to make really individual mosaic designs.

11

# 2 DESIGNING MOSAICS

## Basic equipment

You will need the following materials and tools to design mosaics. These items will not be given again in the list of materials.

- ◆ Copying, squared and tracing paper
- ◆ Carbon paper
- ◆ Ruler, set square, pair of compasses
- ◆ Pencil
- ◆ Water-soluble fine-line ink pen
- ◆ Crayon or artist's paints
- ◆ Scissors and cutter
- ◆ Masking tape

In antiquity, making a mosaic was teamwork, with every step being performed by a specialist. The *Pictor Imaginarius* designed the template. Then the *Pictor Parietarius* transferred this onto the backing material, for which the *Calis Coctor* and the *Pavimentarius* were responsible. The stones were broken by the *Lapidarius* and fitted together by the *Tessellarius*. The *Musearius* created the complex mosaic patterns and the figures. Nowadays, mosaic artists do all the steps themselves. However, it is worth looking at the ancient examples, since over time, set patterns have arisen that were formulated by the Romans in various working methods. The most important is the '*Opus Vermiculatum*'.

Mosaics are inevitably influenced by fashion: the Romans, for example, wanted geometric patterns and representations of figures in keeping with the rising of Christianity, first on light and then on colourful backgrounds. The beginning of the 20th century saw the use of broken ceramic pieces under the influence of the Spanish architect Antonio Gaudí.

In this section, you will learn what to look out for when designing mosaics, including the style and form of the representation as well as flow when laying the tesserae, and the use of colour and grout.

It is best to make the design in the original size and in colour

# PREPARING THE DESIGN

A mosaic is not a painted picture over which an angular grouting grid is laid. Instead, making a mosaic involves filling a complicated surface with the most simple of shapes. However, a design must be drawn out on paper first using colour (coloured crayons or watercolours) or at least a pencil.

When making mosaics, the following two guidelines should be used: 'Bigger things are simpler' and 'Drawing is about leaving things out'. It is best always to stick to the design, which should be carefully drawn, as making subsequent changes to the design when laying the mosaic are usually highly time-consuming.

When designing, you need to take into consideration the size of the stones in relation to the size of the picture. In theory, you can make almost any design in any size. In practice, though, it is clear that a stone cannot be endlessly split and made smaller, be it due to the material itself or for reasons of time and cost. If you have a limited surface available to you for your mosaic, you cannot put in as much as you may want to or work in a very detailed way.

## Advice

◆  For the indirect method (see page 38 onwards), the design drawn with a pencil also serves as the surface for laying the mosaic. The bigger your picture, the thicker the paper you should use. For smaller pieces up to around 20cm (8in) square, normal writing paper (80gsm) is sufficient; for larger pieces that cannot be laid using the sandwich procedure (see Wall and Floor Assembly, page 42), the paper should be 90–120gsm.

◆  Designing a mosaic is one thing, but the task of transferring it is another matter entirely. A mosaic is not painted but laid. This is why it is important to work in a rough way. If you have been used to fine drawings and detail until now, you will need to adapt to this.

◆  Try not to learn about the art of mosaics too quickly. Take time with the preparation, with the design of the mosaic, the choice of colour and the lines when laying the stones.

EXPERT TIPS

### Enlarging or reducing without a copier
If you do not have access to a copier, you can enlarge templates using a grid. It takes a bit longer and requires some practice, but is a good alternative on a rainy Sunday when the copy shop is closed and you really want to do something creative. Draw out a grid on a piece of paper (which should be as big as the original size of the mosaic) in the stated grid dimensions. Use squared or graph paper. Once you have drawn out the grid, the template can be transferred square by square. By using a soft pencil (HB), you can quickly correct a stroke if it is not straight.

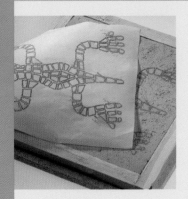

### Transferring designs for direct laying
Designs can easily be transferred to a piece of wood, for example, using carbon paper, but what happens with damp mortar? You will need to use a water-soluble ink pen to transfer the design to tracing paper and then lay this onto the damp mortar with the design side downwards. The pen will then be transferred. If it is important that the mosaic does not appear reversed. Trace the design again on the other side of the tracing paper. Leave the tracing paper briefly once more on the damp mortar. The design can only be transferred once. If necessary, cover some of the areas.

# METHODS OF LAYING

## Advice

◆ The way the tesserae are laid is known as the '*opus*'. The word comes from the Latin and means 'a work'. As well as the most well-known, there are many different handed-down opera, such as *opus sectile*, which is similar to inlaid work; *opus lapilli* and *opus spicatum*, which are different types of pebble mosaic; or *opus segmentatum*, made from a pattern of small and large tesserae in the same colour.

◆ You can compare the inner lines of a motif (see Step 2 of the Step-by-Step Instructions) to the contour lines on a topographical map. When representing a figure, they will be dictated by the shape of the body and also to a large degree by the muscular system, for example, in the case of a human figure, the rounding of the stomach and breast. You will work inwards from these lines.

## Opus vermiculatum

The name comes from '*vermiculus*', meaning 'little worm'. With this method, the rows of stones are laid in a string next to one another. Angular and regular cut stones are used. The size of the individual stones depends on the material available and on the desired level of detail.

The motif is outlined against the background surface by at least one row in the background colour. Thus difficult diagonal cuts are deflected in the uniform background surface. Between the motif and the background is a constant, equal layer of grout. The remaining background is either laid in the *opus vermiculatum* as well or in the *opus tesselatum*.

The motif itself is also laid in the opus vermiculatum, making the figures look very effective (see step-by-step instructions). The individual stones sometimes have different shapes and sizes. The laying technique is often painstaking and detailed.

## Step-by-step instructions

### First lay the main outer contours

1 The main outer contours of a mosaic form the basic structure of the picture. These are laid first as continuous outlines. Preferably basic-shaped stones should be used.

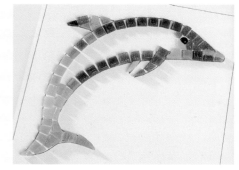

### Then lay the inner contours

2 Next come the inner contours, that is, the contours that come inside a body. The process ensures that the flow fits the body shape and does not run counter to it. In this way, an anatomically natural-looking structure is formed. Wherever possible, this should be done with basic-shaped stones.

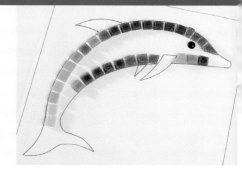

### Keep forming the background until completed

3 Now lay the other parts of the motif, as well as the border. For a straight edge to the border, try to use the factory-finished edge to the material. Then form the background with the stones outlining either the motifs where possible or alternatively, give the background its own flow, e.g. parallel to the edge of the picture.

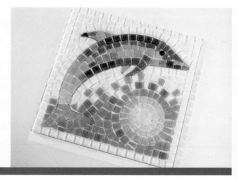

## Opus incertum

The name comes from 'incertum', which means 'uncertain, irregular or disordered'. This method is also called opus palladium or the polygonal laying method.

The material is cut into irregular shapes and sizes. The width of the gaps can vary considerably: the gaps should be of an equal width only between the motif and the background or between the individually coloured areas. This method of laying gives a light, playful effect and a lively, random design. It is also very good for filling remaining areas.

The opus incertum is the most free-form method of covering a surface. However, it can appear wearying over large areas, when used alone. This method of laying is very suitable for beginners who still need to practise the cutting of stones, since it is quick and easy to produce and it is not important to achieve an exact shape.

## Opus quadratum

This method of laying is also known as opus regulatum or the grid method. Most industrial, ready-made tessarae today are laid in a continuous grid formation using the chessboard method of laying (similar to laying tiles). However, this method is only suitable for very large areas, since details will be lost in small areas (like low-pixel photos). Computer mosaics use this technique. The tesserae are not worked on and the grout gaps are close together, giving rise to cross gaps and forming a regular grid of horizontal and vertical rows. The opus quadratum used alone can have a slightly mechanistic effect.

## Opus tesselatum

The name comes from 'tessella', meaning 'little cube', and this opus is in one or more colours, with mostly geometric mosaics from stone or marble cubes, which are all the same size (up to 2cm or ¾in). The opus tesselatum is usually used for backgrounds. It differs from the opus quadratum in that there are no cross gaps. Instead, the stones (and the gaps) are arranged slightly offset from one another. This should be followed over the whole mosaic, otherwise the overall effect will be disrupted.

# DESIGNING WITH COLOUR

## Mosaic palette

The colour palette for mosaic materials is limited and, unlike painting, new colours cannot be made by mixing colours. Commercially, only a few shades of red, pink, orange and yellow are available, yet there are lots of shades of blue and green. Metallic tesserae, such as shimmering silver, copper and gold, are also on offer. Test out the effect of the colours on a few patterns: the closer the mosaic is to the window, the stronger the colours will appear. When hung between two windows or directly opposite a window, the colours will appear darker. Electric light can also alter the appearance of colours. It is therefore a good idea to look at the colour pattern at different times of day and under different light sources.

## Colour selection and stylization

With a limited colour palette, the choice of colours is all the more important and some stylization is essential, for instance by working with warm and cold colours or strong and weak shades. A motif created in warm colours will stand out very clearly against a cold background. If, however, the same colour temperature is selected for each, a more harmonious and subtle impression will be achieved. Different effects can also be obtained using light and dark, as shown in the top two examples on page 18. Here, the same bright colours were set in both a white and a black background, the latter making the colours shine more brightly.

The example of the dolphin shown left demonstrates how the selection of colour and material influences the effect of the mosaic. Above, it is made from cool, glass stones, and below, in contrast, from muted natural stones.

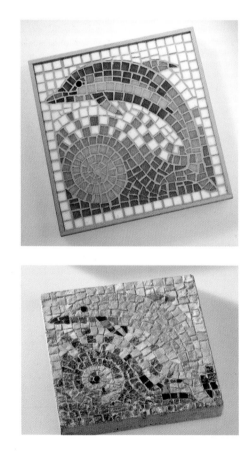

# Colour

Colour is used to denote the pure appearance within the colour spectrum, such as red, yellow, green and blue. You are able to choose between primary, secondary and tertiary colours. Primary colours are the colours that cannot be made by mixing: yellow, red and blue (black and white do not count as colours). The secondary colours are formed from mixing primary colours: green (from yellow and blue), orange (from red and yellow) and violet (from blue and red). All other colour mixes give tertiary colours. With mosaics, it is not possible to mix colours, unless you work in the style of the pointillists, such as Georges Seurat, and achieve coloured areas by using a combination of colours laid together in small sections, such as orange from yellow and red.

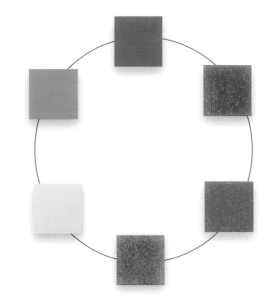

Colours that are opposite each other on the colour wheel form complementary colours, for example, yellow and violet, which combined achieve the highest colour intensity.

Colours that form a triangle on the colour wheel are known as a colour triad. This is very interesting, since all the colours stand very much in contrast to one another. By combining shades that stand next to each other on the colour wheel, for instance, red, orange and yellow, analogue colours are achieved. This combination is harmonious and natural, with the colours blending into one another.

## Tone

The tone of a colour determines how light or dark it is. In mosaics, the distinction is made between light, medium and dark. Different colours can have the same tone – for instance, red and green are equally dark. If a dark tone is next to a light one, it will appear even darker. Tones that are the same have a very harmonious effect and there is very little difference between the colour shading (see the example below).

## Intensity

The colour intensity shows whether a colour is muted or bright – in other words, the strength and weakness of the colour. A strong tessera will appear more radiant if it is next to a weak-coloured one and two complementary colours together have the greatest intensity.

## Temperature

The colour temperature refers to the association of warmth and cold. Generally, sunny red, orange and yellow tones are considered warm, while sea colours, such as blue and green, are considered cold. Warm colours make parts of the motif stand out more and give the impression of warmth, comfort and energy. Cold colours, on the other hand, make parts of the motif retract and give the impression of coolness and stability. Cool colours can have a warmer effect if they contain part of a warmer colour, such as yellowy green versus bluey green.

## Tips & Tricks

◆ Colour mixes in the pointillism style only work when they are made up of lots of little pieces placed together and viewed from a distance. Remember this principle when you are using this method.

◆ Take advantage of the calming yet interesting effect of using the same tones when forming large surface areas – the tessarae in every batch always vary a little, so if they are mixed and randomly distributed prior to laying, the result will have greater visual interest as well as depth.

◆ Always take a step back when viewing your work to get an impression of the whole mosaic. If you have a digital camera, look at your work on the display, since this will give you a good overview of the piece.

# GROUT AND GROUT COLOURS

## Grout colours

The grouting of the mosaic has a considerable influence on the finished piece, which is why the grout should also be selected when devising the design. You can also work without grout when laying mosaics, but often the grout completes the mosaic and also has a practical use: it makes the mosaic more durable. The impression of the picture is determined by the grout, which has the effect of a visible inlaid grid.

A white grout goes well with bright colours and gives emphasis to a light piece. It stands out strongly against a dark surrounding too. Dark and black grouts are good for edging dark tesserae or to brighten up light shades.

If you are unsure, choose a medium shade, such as mid-grey. Grey grouts are neutral and set off all tessarae, apart from grey. They hold the picture together, since grey works well against both light and dark surroundings. As a general rule of thumb, the colour of the grout should be somewhere between the lightest and the darkest shades of the tesserae.

**EXPERT TIP**

**Mixing your own colour of grout**
White grouting compound can be made brightly coloured by adding colour pigments (available both in powder form or dissolved as emulsion). Add the desired colour to the mixed grout and stir well.

As it is difficult to make the same shade a second time, if you are using your own mixed grout, only grout surfaces that are of a size that you can complete with one mix.

# Grout colour palette

A range of grouting compounds are commercially available in all sorts of colours. The coloured ones are usually a bit more expensive, but you can colour white grouting compound yourself using colour pigments (see Expert Tip below opposite). Strongly coloured grouting compounds should only be used with care, since a vivid grout can easily stand out too much against subtly coloured surroundings. Multiple colours of grout should only be used by experienced users, since a clean break between one colour of grout and the next without mixing at the join is difficult to achieve. As a general guideline, the grout should not stand out too much and not be overbearing.

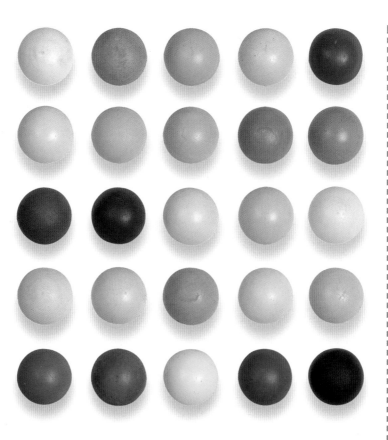

## Tips & Tricks

◆ If you want to use a light grout for your mosaic, yet want to avoid a very visible white grout grid effect, you can use ivory-coloured mortar.

◆ Using dark mortar, such as anthracite or black, comes closest to a look of an ungrouted mosaic. Ignore the shade of the damp grouting compound, since it will become lighter as it dries.

◆ As a general rule, grout a mosaic in its predominant shades, but if there is a very strong colour contrast, grey is the best choice.

## Multiple colours of grout

If grouting with more than one colour, you will need to work in several individual steps. Allow the individually grouted areas to dry a little, making surplus grouting compound easier to wipe away. Start with the darkest colour of grout, since light grout is more difficult to clean again. Do not immediately scrape out surplus grout using a pointed object, but wait until the grouting compound has started to dry out (about 30 minutes). When spreading the grout, use small, flat tools, such as a sponge or paintbrush. It is not all that easy to make a clean break between one colour and the next. Mixing two colours can, however, look quite attractive.

# 3 TOOLS AND EQUIPMENT

## Basic equipment

You will need these tools to break up the mosaic materials. Always have the most suitable and your preferred tools to hand, as they will not be included again in the list of materials.

- Mosaic nippers
- Glass cutter and breaking pincers (for glass and ceramic)
- Glass nibbling pincers (for industrial glass)
- Tile cutter (for ceramic)
- Mosaic hammer and awl (for natural stone)
- Mosaic hammer and awl with hard metal coating or smalti nippers (for smalti)
- Plastic or fabric bag and hammer (for breaking up Gaudí-style)
- Plank to take the impact or a metal ruler
- Glazier's pliers
- Hand brush or small brush (to clear fallen pieces)
- Protective clothing (dust mask, safety goggles and gloves)

A range of different tools can be used for cutting mosaic materials. The most versatile are mosaic nippers, which every workshop should have. They can be used to cut glass, as well as ceramic and natural stone. Depending on the type of material, special tools are also available that make cutting, which is often time-consuming, considerably easier. These include glass cutters, although their name can be a little misleading, as they are also good for ceramic, as well as glass nibbling pincers. The latter are exclusively for use with glass, making them a good alternative to mosaic nippers, and they are also easy for beginners to use.

When working with natural stone, a hammer and awl are used. The awl needs to be firmly anchored in a wooden or concrete base. Working with these professional tools requires a lot of practice, but they can be very useful, since they can be used to break up expensive smalti (for these, the hammer and awl need to be coated with a hard metal), small pebbles or glass plates prepared with the glass cutter.

Mosaic nippers – indispensable for mosaic artists

Glass cutter – a somewhat misleading name, as they also cut ceramic

# Important TOOLS

### Glass cutter and breaking pincers

One cannot be used without the other, since breaking pincers can only be used on scored glass. A glass cutter has a small diamond wheel at the front and is used free-hand or with the help of a metal ruler or support board (see page 24). It is drawn over the mosaic material (remember to use cutting fluid). Even curved cuts are possible. Finally, the scored material is divided with the breaking pincers. Breaking pincers and glass cutters are available from DIY stores and specialist glass suppliers. Make sure that the wheels are of a high quality and made from hard metal. Unlike working with glass breaking pincers and mosaic nippers, a glass cutter can be used to make long, exact cuts. It is a very versatile tool that can be used for glass mosaic stones and stoneware as well as ceramic.

### Please note:

You should wear safety goggles whenever you are cutting, as the mosaic material is prone to splintering, which could hurt you. If you are cutting for prolonged periods, wear a dust mask too!

### Advice

◆ Always have cutting fluid to hand to oil the glass cutter wheels. It penetrates the surface when cutting, ensures a clean break and absorbs the cut glass particles so that the wheel moves freely. This considerably prolongs its life.

### Tips & Tricks

◆ Practise makes perfect. At the start, you'll find it difficult to cut mosaic stones, but over time and with experience, you will perfect your ability to the point where you will be equally able to cut a triangle or a strip from a mosaic stone. Just keep practising!

## Glass nibbling pincers

Glass nibbling pincers are suitable for glass mosaics up to a thickness of 4mm (5/32in). They are not suitable for stoneware. The tool has a long handle and two hard metal cutting discs. Some glass nibbling pincers have a practical collecting bag to catch the material after it has been cut up. Take care when removing the pieces of glass from the bag, as you can easily cut yourself on them. It is a good idea to shake the glass pieces out of the bag.

Even beginners can quickly and easily make triangles, narrow strips and more using glass nibbling pincers (see page 26). However, only short cuts are possible (industrial mosaic up to 2cm or ¾in), otherwise it is better to use a glass cutter.

Important tools continued

Important tools
continued

## Mosaic nippers

Mosaic nippers are the most versatile of cutting tools. Every mosaic workshop should have them. Their jaws are strengthened with a hard metal and they can cut every type of mosaic material. The long handle provides good leverage. The nippers are recognizable by the spring between their handles. You can also use them to make circles and other curved shapes (see page 27).

## Tips & Tricks

◆ If you are going to start at the edge, as opposed to cutting straight across the middle, then it is better to use mosaic nippers. The angle at which the nippers are used corresponds to the slant of the cut.

## Tile cutters

There are two types of cutters: handheld and table-top. Their function is, however, the same. The material is firstly scored with a grooved wheel, then placed between the breaking jaws and divided by applying pressure (see page 25).

Small handheld tile cutters are suitable for stoneware tiles up to an edge length of 15cm (6in) and a thickness of 6mm (¼in). For larger formats and thicknesses, table-top tile cutters are used. With these, the wheel and breaking jaws are attached to a long handle. This gives greater leverage when breaking the tiles. The pieces that have been cut can be adjusted with ordinary nippers or with mosaic nippers.

## Mosaic hammer and awl (turn-up tools)

The hammer and awl (also known as turn-up tools) are traditional mosaic tools that are especially suitable for cutting natural stone or smalti. This cutting technique does require a bit of practise, as the mosaic hammer should not touch the awl when splitting the stone (see page 26).

The awl has a sharp blade and sits with its shaft firmly in a wooden base (such as a tree trunk sawn to the correct working height) or is fixed into another stable base. The mosaic hammer has a rounded shape and two flat, tapering ends. It weighs 450g (1lb) or 950g (2lb 2oz). Both ends of the hammer can be used for striking. When working with smalti, both the hammer and awl are coated with a hard metal.

## Hammer and fabric bag

An ordinary, household hammer that weighs about 400g (14oz) can be used to break porcelain, stoneware, crockery, vases and so on into manageable pieces. The material should, however, be placed in a fabric or plastic bag to minimize the risk of injury.

This technique was very popular in Spanish Art Nouveau. Many of Antonio Gaudí's works, for instance, are covered with random-cut porcelain.

## Tips & Tricks

◆ Apart from the hammer and awl, you can also work with mosaic nippers on natural stone. It is often easier to remove raised edges with these than with using a hammer.

◆ For large surfaces, industrially made natural stone tesserae are good, since striking larger stones by hand with a hammer and awl is very time-consuming. For smaller pieces, stones that you have broken yourself should be used, as the small irregularities that arise when splitting bring added interest to the mosaic and make it something unique.

◆ To achieve equal-sized cubes of natural stone, strips can be sawn from a sheet using a wet cutting machine (electric saw with diamond-set blade and water cooling). You can also have them cut by a stonemason or a supplier of natural stone materials.

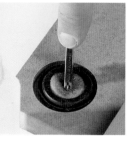

# USING THE TOOLS

## Cutting with a glass cutter and breaking pincers

First of all, the material is scored with the glass cutter along the cutting line. Some glass cutters have an oiling device on the cutting wheel, otherwise oil the wheel after every two or three cuts using an oil-soaked piece of felt. Then draw the tool once over the mosaic stone (do not saw backwards and forwards) to score a line in the surface. If the pressure was not sufficient, the process can be repeated. However, you then risk the stone not breaking cleanly. Very accurate cuts can be made using a glass cutter. Make sure that you achieve a right angle between the position of the glass cutter and that of the material.

Place the prepared stone between the jaws of the breaking pincers. Hold the breaking pincers so that the white stripe appears at the top and points in the same direction as the direction of cutting. Then squeeze together slowly and equally. The stones break really well if they are held firmly at the front cutting end between the thumb and index finger.

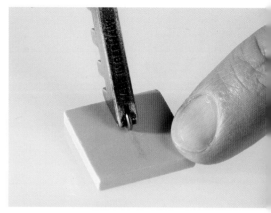

**Cutting in half and quarters using a support board**
A suitable support board is useful for accurately cutting in half or quarters. Place the stone into the support board (in the photo a stone is being cut in half). Score the stone with the glass cutter (smear with cutting fluid beforehand), then break the stone with the breaking pincers. To cut the half into quarters, place the stone in the support board again and score crossways, then break.

**Make your own support board**
You can easily make a support board yourself. You need a right-angled piece of wood, such as MDF about 20 x 10cm (8 x 4in) and three thin rectangular pieces. The planks are as thick as your mosaic stone and approximately 2cm (¾in) wide, and are the same length as the base. First, stick one long and one short plank to the two sides of the piece of wood at right angles to each other. Nail or glue the third plank along the long side slightly overlapping (depending on the size of the stone and the glass cutter used). When cut, the pressure on the stone will come from the underneath planks, while the top one provides the right distance for cutting in half.

## Working with tile cutters

Draw the cutting line on the tile or measure out using the integrated ruler. Then draw the wheel swiftly and with strong pressure over the cutting line (do not saw backwards and forwards). Now and again, treat the wheel with cutting oil (see Cutting with a glass cutter and breaking pincers and second Tip opposite).

Then place the scored material between the breaking jaws of the tile cutter, so that pressure is exerted on both sides of the scored line. From below, an awl presses against the cut, and from above, two jaws break the tile apart. A leverage effect is created through the guide rails that are usually fairly long and are used for breaking. This can be an advantage with thick tiles. For smaller pieces, handheld tile cutters can also be used (see Advice on the right). To cut larger tiles with an edge length of over 15cm (6in), the table-top tile cutter should always be used.

## Advice

◆ Handheld tile cutters consist of a wooden or metal handle that drives a moving wheel at the tip. The quality of the cutters (and their price) depends mainly upon the quality of the wheel. Normal metal wheels are cheaper, but the material is also softer and has a shorter life than the more expensive, hard metal wheels. Unlike table-top tile cutters, the wheel usually cannot be changed.

## Cutting roughly and randomly

To cut tiles or porcelain roughly, a hammer may be used. Place the material in a plastic or fabric bag and lightly hit with the hammer. The bag will reduce the risk of injury. As you go along, remove pieces that are sufficiently small from the bag and continue working with the rest. Particular pieces can later be cut more accurately with a glass cutter and the breaking pincers or nipped off with mosaic nippers. If you want to break up a lot of material with the hammer, you can do this on a block of wood on thick, soft underlay. This acts as a sound absorber.

Using the tools
continued

Using the tools
continued

## Advice

◆ Smalti are either cut using a hammer and awl or with special nippers. Their shape is similar to that of glass nibbling pincers, but they are more stable to work with.

## Tips & Tricks

◆ Do not try to achieve a conical shape from a square stone that is almost the right shape by chipping away tiny triangles. It will only produce wastage. Always cut in such a way that you can use the leftover pieces of tile as well.

◆ Each material has its own properties that will affect its ability to split. Do not become disheartened by mistakes. Skilful use of the hammer and awl requires some practise.

# Cutting with glass nibbling pincers

Glass nibbling pincers can only make short cuts into glass stones up to 4mm ($^5/_{32}$in) thick. They are not suitable for use with other materials and for gnawing off small corners (for example, cutting an octagon from a square tesserae).

To cut the material, hold it at a right angle to the wheel and place the nippers approximately two-thirds across the material (not exactly in the middle). For better leverage, hold the handle as far back as possible and squeeze firmly.

Pincers are good for beginners, because they are easy to use in comparison with a glass cutter or mosaic nippers and work well even on first attempts. For longer cuts, a glass cutter should be used.

To lay round-shaped mosaics, conical tesserae are needed. To make these, cut a square-shaped stone in half so that you have a rectangle. This can then easily be cut on a slant into three pieces (see also the first Tip on the left).

# Splitting using a hammer and awl

To split natural stone, for example, by using a hammer and awl, place the material on the awl, holding it between your thumb and index finger so that its blade points in the direction that the material is to be split.

Try not to swing the hammer down onto the material, but rather let it drop naturally. The material will break from the weight of the hammer hitting it. Be careful to ensure that the mosaic hammer does not touch the awl when hitting, which would blunt the blades.

Every cube can be cut in half, quarters or eighths again until the desired size is reached. To ensure a clean cut, make a single, sharp hit with the hammer. If several hits are necessary, from possibly hitting too timidly, the result is often an irregular cut.

## Working with circular shapes using mosaic nippers

Unlike working with paper and scissors, where every shape can be directly cut out, when cutting mosaic materials, some intermediate steps are necessary in order to achieve a round or oval shape. In order to achieve a circle, for example, you must first make an octagon and then keep nipping off the edges of the stone. The shape will be nice and round if you finish off by working with glazier's pliers.

In classical mosaic work, there are no round mosaic stones; they are replaced by octagons that look very similar or by individual shapes placed together.

## Please note:

Sharp splinters can form when cutting up glass mosaics. Never remove these with your bare hands — always use a brush to avoid risk of injury.

## Advice

◆ Glazier's pliers can be used for nibbling away curved edges on ceramic (as well as stoneware) and glass, and also for finishing off remaining, small corners. They come in different widths (adjustable depending on the size of the curve). Professional tools have very durable, hard metal jaws, a locking screw (to prevent the jaws from being totally pressed together) and a return spring, which serves to open the hard metal jaws automatically.

◆ Other possibilities for cutting mosaic stones can be found on pages 60, 80 and 84.

## Step-by-step instructions

### Cutting an octagon

**1** In order to make a tesserae round, the corners must be nipped away using mosaic nippers. First an octagon is formed by nipping off the four corners. To do this, place the nippers at the corner of the stone and squeeze together.

### Finishing off the shape

**2** Keep finishing off the shape (continuing to cut off the corners all round) until a circle is formed. By just working with mosaic nippers, the shape will not be completely round. It can now be further rounded using glazier's pliers.

### Fine work using glazier's pliers

**3** Glazier's pliers are not used like pincers, but more like a file – the handles are not squeezed together, but the jaws of the pliers (the inner edges are ribbed) are drawn over the edge of the material. The upper jaw files the material, while the lower one provides the right support. Hold the stone gently and take the pliers downwards using a turning movement.

The direct method is the traditional procedure for laying mosaics. As far back as 300BC in Greece, natural stone cubes or pebbles were pushed into a 'thick bed' made from three different granular layers of plaster. Nowadays, a thin bed of cement-based mortar is usually used and, apart from detailed creations on walls and in rooms, the materials are stuck into mobile bases, such as Styrodur®, plasterboard, aerate concrete, glass or wood. The advantage of the thin-bed process is that the spreading thickness is just 2mm (³/₃₂in). However, this means that any unevenness in the background or different thicknesses of material cannot be evened out. This is why the direct method is suitable for creating relief pictures, but not for making table tops or other level surfaces. Grouting the mosaic, by filling the gaps between the individual tesserae, can be dispensed with on visual grounds in the pure art of mosaics.

## Basic equipment

You need the following materials and tools for working in the direct method. Have them ready, as they will not be included in the list of materials.

- Measuring and drawing tools
- Plaster mixing cup and spoon (for mixing grout and glue)
- Plasterer's spatula, small trowel (for applying glue and grout)
- Flat paintbrush (for spreading the key)
- Grout rubber, sponge board or round brush (for grouting)
- Bucket of cold water, sponge and sponge cloth
- Rubber gloves
- Protective clothing (dust mask and safety goggles)

Direct method – a mosaic with a relief surface structure

# IMPORTANT EQUIPMENT

## Base and primer

Not all materials bind equally well with others. It is important that the base does not move, making the following materials very suitable for use as a base: wood (MDF or blockboard, at least 1.5cm or 5/8in thick), concrete, plaster, Styrodur®, plasterboard and ceramic. The base and the mosaic material should bind strongly together, which is why a slightly rough surface that is neither too porous nor too hard to absorb any moisture is ideal. The best properties are offered by concrete and plaster. Wood and clay pots, on the other hand, have a very porous outer surface, while porcelain and glass are too smooth, which is why these bases must be pretreated with a primer. A universal primer (water-based), available from DIY stores, is suitable for this. By painting on with a brush, these adhesive primers seal a surface that is too porous as well as provide a flat surface with a key, due to the addition of quartz sand.

With very porous surfaces, the primer can often be thinned with water in a 1:1 ratio, which will make it easier to paint on. Allow the primer to dry well (at least an hour).

## Measuring and drawing tools

You will find the following tools useful for geometry when transferring the design: ruler, tape measure, folding ruler and compasses (see Tip on page 84). Some tape measures have a fold-out pin for marking the mid-point of a circle. Pull out the tape and set it at the required length. At the end of somes tapes there is a hole in which a pen can be inserted. This means that you can draw circles with a diameter of up to 6m (6½yd) (for large pieces, you will need help with this). For small pieces, such as transferring representations of figures, carbon paper is good. A protractor and set square are indispensable for drawing out and checking right-angled corners.

## Advice

◆ Remove old paint before priming or at least create a key using coarse sandpaper. Remember to follow the manufacturer's instructions.

## Tips & Tricks

◆ Concrete or Styrodur® is an ideal base for tables planned for outdoor use. Make the concrete top as a flat cast, as described on page 43 onwards. The larger the table top, the more stable the reinforcing iron wire grid placed in the middle should be (see page 44, Step 6).

◆ Thin metal or tin are unsuitable as a base for mosaic work, although they are quite stable in themselves. As these materials typically flex, they would cause the stones to come loose. If you have found an old table in a flea market that only has a thin metal top, put a second, inflexible wooden top on top of it.

◆ As a general rule, it is more difficult to get a good contact between mosaic and metal or plastic than between mosaic and wood, ceramic or concrete.

# THE RIGHT ADHESIVE

## Please note:

Remember to wear protective clothing when working with epoxy resin adhesive (safety goggles and gloves) and change out of dirty work clothes straight away. If you are working for any period of time with cement-based, thin-bed mortar, you should wear protective gloves. If it should come into contact with your eyes, wash out immediately with water and consult a doctor.

## Advice

◆ Many manufacturers supply additional substances that can be mixed into the adhesive to make it malleable, water-repellent and with a higher degree of adhesion. But generally these substances are not needed.

◆ Thin-bed adhesive is also available as quick-drying cement. This is not normally suitable for working with mosaics, as corrections often need to be made. Once it has hardened, improvements are very difficult to make.

The right adhesive to choose for fixing tesserae is dependent on three components: which material will be stuck to which base and where the mosaic will be used.

Most frequently, cement-based, thin-bed mortar is used (tile adhesive). The powder is mixed with water in the plaster mixing cup. It is available for use both indoors and outdoors (frost-resistant) and is suitable for all bases. Very porous or smooth non-porous surfaces must be pre-prepared with a key. For increased adhesion, needed especially for bases such as Styropor® and porcelain, a flexible thin-bed mortar can be used. This adhesive consists of a powder with special elements, filling compounds and flexible synthetic substances.

Cement-based adhesives are available in a variety of colours, such as white and grey. The shade of colour should be chosen according to the subsequent colour of grout: if the grout is grey or another dark colour, use grey, but with light colours, use white. Adhesive can be used for both direct and indirect methods and is very suitable for mosaic objects, because the pieces sit well in it and do not slip.

Dispersion adhesive is a soft, dispersion-based, mixed adhesive and is especially suitable for non-porous bases, such as thick, smooth concrete and tiles. It is only suitable for indoor use. Any excess glue on the mosaic must be wiped away immediately after laying.

Epoxy resin adhesive is a dual component, resin-based adhesive, which consists of a proprietary paste and a soft resin. It is especially used where cement-based mortar is insufficiently load-bearing or not durable and where hygiene is important, such as in kitchens. The adhesive is practically insoluble and sticks to any base. However, extreme care should be taken when working with it, as this adhesive is an allergen. It is only used for the direct method.

PVA adhesive (polyvinyl acetate) is often recommended. This is a white craft glue (wood glue). This adhesive is available in water-soluble and waterproof versions. The latter is suitable for sticking mosaic tesserae using the direct method. A disadvantage of this adhesive is that its consistency is very fluid. Unevenness in the material or base cannot be evened out with it.

Silicone adhesives are primarily used for sticking items to glass. They are clear-drying, transparent adhesives with a soft consistency. A disadvantage of this adhesive is that any adhesive or silicone spilt on the material is difficult to remove. This adhesive is mainly applied with a glue gun.

# GROUTING MOSAICS

## Important tools

Various tools are required when grouting mosaics: a plaster mixing cup for mixing the grouting compound and an old spoon, a plasterer's spatula for applying it to the mosaic, depending on the base and the size of the work, and a small trowel or round brush. In the case of flat mosaics, when working the grout into the gaps, you will need to use a grout rubber or a sponge board. Mosaic objects are grouted with a paintbrush, sponge or by hand (wear rubber gloves). To clean the mosaic, you will need a sponge, a bucket of cold water, a sponge cloth and a soft, lint-free rag for the final polish. You should wear gloves when grouting and washing off the mosaic.

## Advice

◆ Not all grouting compounds are frost-resistant and some are therefore only suitable for indoor use. Follow the manufacturer's instructions.

## Tips & Tricks

◆ You can get special tiling sponges from tile specialists that have a fine, dense structure and absorb water as well as mortar. This makes the mosaic easier to clean than with an ordinary kitchen sponge.

◆ Ready-made grouting compounds are available that are actually difficult to apply and later remove from the material. Products that combine adhesive and mortar are not recommended. They frequently have insufficient adhesion and are difficult to remove from mosaics.

◆ Wide grouting compound can also be used for fine gaps. It is often easier to remove from the surface.

## Grouting compound

Grouting compound is a cement-based powder and special filling compound (quartz sand) that is mixed with water. It contains less cement than tile adhesive and cannot therefore be used in place of this. Grouting compound is used to fill gaps between mosaic tesserae. When mixed with water, a soft, smooth mortar is obtained that should be free of lumps. Follow the mix ratio given by the manufacturer.

Grouting compound is available in a range of different colours, such as grey, anthracite, black, ivory and white. Coloured grout can also be bought from DIY stores or tile specialists, or you can colour white grout yourself (see Expert Tip on page 18). There is a difference between narrow (or fine) and wide grouting compound. Narrow grouting compound is for gaps up to around 4mm (⅛in), whereas wide grouting compound is for larger gaps. In the latter, the proportion of quartz sand is higher, which prevents cracks occurring when drying.

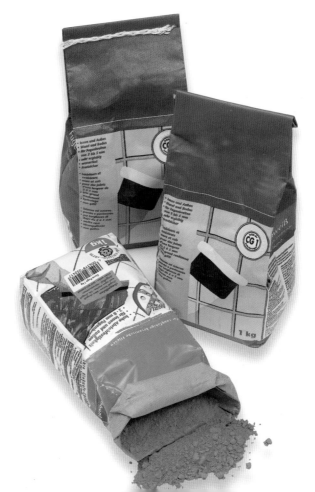

◆ Always add the water first to the plaster mixing cup, then the glue or the grouting compound powder. When working, take care not to cause dust clouds, as the dust can be harmful for the lungs (always wear a dust mask).

◆ The adhesive should be soft but not dripping. You can alter its consistency by adding water to the adhesive powder.

◆ Only mix as much adhesive as you can work with in a period of 20 minutes. Follow the manufacturer's instructions on the working time.

## Tips & Tricks

◆ You can also use a ready-mixed dispersion adhesive. This has the advantage that you can keep taking a small amount without having continually to mix up new adhesive.

◆ Be careful not to soil the surface of the mosaic tesserae with adhesive. Wipe away marks immediately with a damp sponge.

# Step-by-step instructions

### Prepare the base

**1** Prime the base, if necessary, with an adhesive primer (see page 29). Tile layers use this too to make mosaics on sheet rock bases. You can buy the primer from DIY stores.

### Transfer the design

**2** After drying, transfer the design using carbon paper onto the base (where necessary, fix with masking tape so that it does not slip). For slightly curved bases, it is best to cut out the pieces of the motif individually and transfer them. Then cut the mosaic tesserae accurately (see Tools and Equipment from page 20 onwards).

### Mix the adhesive

**3** If you do not have a stock of stones ready, mix some adhesive in a plaster mixing cup. Use commercially available tile adhesive in a ratio of 3:1, that is, three parts adhesive powder stirred into one part water, avoiding lumps. Leave the compound to rest briefly (around 5 minutes) and then stir again.

### Apply the adhesive

**4** Apply the adhesive about 2mm (3/32in) thick using a spatula or modelling spatula to the part of the base that you want to lay first. If your mosaic is a patterned one, you should work on this first, then the background (see page 14). The stone should sit fully in the adhesive, but it should not run over the top of the stone.

### Lay the mosaic stones

**5** In order to achieve a level surface, carefully press the mosaic with a smooth object. If you want to take a break, remove the excess adhesive. Make sure that none of the stones are touching one another and leave a gap between the individual tesserae of at least 1mm (1/32in).

### Mix the grouting compound

**6** Allow the completed mosaic to dry for at least 24 hours and then grout. Use the correct grouting compound. Here it is one for narrow gaps (see page 31). Mix the grouting compound with clean water to make a soft, light, lump-free compound (ratio about 1:2.75, following the manufacturer's instructions). Spoon the grout powder into the water.

### Grouting

**7** Press the grouting compound over the area into the gaps using an empty washing-up liquid bottle, a trowel or a sponge (for flat bases) or a thick, round brush (for uneven surfaces). Then spread grout several times in all directions over the whole of the mosaic. Leave to stand for around 10 minutes until the grouting compound begins to dry at the edges

### Remove excess grout

**8** Using the sponge board (for uneven surfaces, use a sponge), remove the grouting compound. Now go over the mosaic with a well-squeezed sponge to remove excess grout and smooth the gaps. Do not wash the grouting compound out of the gaps and keep rinsing out the sponge well.

### Polish off with a sponge cloth

**9** The mosaic has so far only been roughly cleaned. Now it will be polished. After cleaning with the sponge, a light layer of grout film will remain on the mosaic, which should be removed after around 5–10 minutes with a damp, well-squeezed sponge cloth. Slowly wash over the mosaic several times in all directions and keep rinsing out the cloth well.

### Further treatment

**10** After about 30 minutes–1 hour (when the grouting compound has dried out), wipe the remaining soiling off with a dry cloth. When the gaps have completely dried out, polish the mosaic again stone by stone. If necessary, use a standard floor cleaner.

## Advice

◆ Wash all your working implements with water. Do not pour the dirty water down the drain, as cement can block it up.

◆ If, in spite of a thorough cleaning, the film of cement is still apparent, you can treat your mosaic with a cement film remover (from DIY stores or tile specialists) about a week later. This will dissolve the film of cement, remains of the mortar and any lime deposits (do not, therefore, use with marble and limestone mosaics). Moisten the surface of your work and apply the product with a sponge (for heavy soiling, use the remover undiluted, otherwise dilute 1:1 with water). The acid can also be worked in using a brush. Leave to work for 2–3 minutes, then wash off with lots of water until it is free of residues. Be sure to wear protective gloves and safety goggles when doing this.

# FINISHING THE EDGES

## With tesserae

When the edge of the base is to be created using tesserae, it must be made first (before laying the mosaic), as making the border will increase the size of the diameter of the base by twice the thickness of the stones. Spread adhesive primer around the edge and, after sticking on the tesserae, leave to dry for at least 24 hours. When gluing, it is best to use a flexible tile adhesive. The stones are really easy to stick on when the base is upside down on the work surface (line with foil), because this ensures that they are pressed level with the table and will all be stuck at the same height.

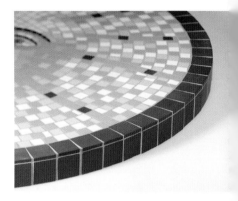

## With metal

Metal frames look the nicest when they are made by a metal-worker using flat steel. Have the frame made before laying the mosaic, especially for round surfaces, since it will rarely be totally circular. Then cut out the base to an exact fit. Secure the metal frame with at least four screws at the sides of the base.

Metal tape is also available from DIY stores. It is very thin and can be laid around the finished mosaic (screwed tight). It does not, however, make a stable frame and the joints are relatively difficult to seal.

When choosing the frame, the height is calculated from the thickness of the base, plus the height of the mosaic material and the thin bed of mortar (1–2mm) (¹⁄₃₂–³⁄₃₂in).

## With strips of wood

Angular pieces can be framed with strips of wood. There are two ways of doing this: you can make the mosaic and then build a wooden frame around it, or you can stick the frame to the base (which we recommend) and then lay the mosaic (keep wiping down untreated natural wood frames with a dry cloth; painted frames absorb less moisture). When sticking together, paint both the strips of wood and the base with wood glue and fix it all additionally with tiny nails (compress the nails). Two strips the size of the base and two strips the size of the base plus twice the thickness of the strips are needed. Calculate the thickness of the strip as described for the metal frame. To cut, you will need a wood or mitre saw. If the frame is to be painted, do this before fitting the mosaic in.

# DIRECT METHOD USING NETTING

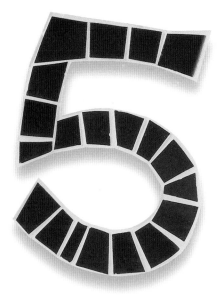

The direct method using netting, glass fibre webbing with a 4mm (³/₃₂in) mesh, is used mainly for practical reasons: you can work on the mosaic on the table and then mount it in its final position afterwards. It's good for when the weather is bad outside, yet you would like to make something attractive to put on the bare outside wall of the house. The netting serves as a temporary base, as with the indirect method on paper (see page 38). But in this case, the tesserae are stuck on with the top side upwards, and very little adhesive is used when sticking the tesserae to the netting so that they will stick well to the mortar afterwards. If you are making a large wall picture, always work in small areas, at the most 50cm (20in) square, so that it is not too heavy and the pieces of the picture stick securely together. It is difficult to bring them together again later. Cut through the netting along a gap using a cutter, try to avoid cutting at an obvious point around the motif, this will ensure that it will not be noticeable later that the picture is made up of several pieces placed together.

## Step-by-step instructions

### Position the drawing

Place the drawing, with transparent film and the netting on top, on a mobile base, such as wood, for example. The film prevents the mosaic from sticking to the background. Secure everything to the base with masking tape so that it does not slip.

**1**

### Laying tesserae

Now lay the tesserae, starting with the main motif (see page 14). Spread just a little adhesive (water-proof wood glue, dispersion adhesive or flexible, cement-based tile adhesive) on the underneath side and press firmly on the stone. Always ensure that the gaps are of an equal width and that the edge is straight.

**2**

### Further work on the mosaic

Once the adhesive has dried, loosen the mosaic from the base. Cut through the netting around the edge of the mosaic using a cutter. This works well with curved shapes too. Then fix the mosaic in its final position by pressing into an even layer of adhesive and packing it down with a rubber hammer. Then grout.

**3**

## Tips & Tricks

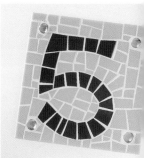

◆ This is what the house number plate in the step-by-step instructions looks like. You will need two stoneware tiles for each colour and four glass nuggets. Stick down using frost-resistant adhesive and grout with white grouting after fixing to the wall of the house.

◆ To avoid slippage when fixing individual pieces on netting to vertical surfaces, insert a nail underneath a large tesserae here and there. When mounting, always start at the top.

◆ When transporting pieces on netting, hold onto each side at the top corners and leave the rest of the surface to fall freely below.

## Pebble tiles

Prepare the wooden frame as described on page 34. Stick on the tessarae using the direct method (see pages 32–33), making the straight and diagonal lines first, then the mirror shards and finally the pebbles.

Cut the mirror glass into strips 1cm (³⁄₈in) wide and nip into irregular pieces using the tile nippers. Cut the tesserae: small triangles (beige), large triangles (white) and four long pieces (cream), then the rest into small, irregular squares. Finally, grout.

**MOTIF SIZE**
Approx. 18cm (7in) square

**MATERIALS**

◆ Piece of wood, 8mm (⁵⁄₁₆in) thick, 18cm (7in) square

◆ Planks of wood, 2mm (³⁄₃₂in) thick, 1cm (³⁄₈in) wide, 4 x approx. 19cm (7½in) long

◆ Pebbles in various colours and sizes

◆ Tinted antique mirrored glass, 10 x 20cm (4 x 8in)

◆ Tesserae: 2 x beige and 8 x cream, 2.5cm (1in) square

◆ Tessera in white, 2cm (¾in) square

◆ Flexible, cement-based adhesive in grey

◆ Grout in grey

◆ Small wood saw

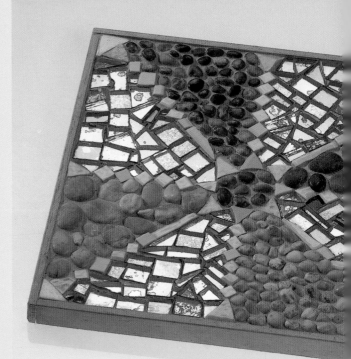

# PROJECTS

**MOTIF SIZE**
Diameters approx. 3.5–7cm (1³⁄₈–2¾in)

**MATERIALS**

◆ Brooches in various sizes

◆ Various colourful, transparent pieces of glass

◆ Silicone adhesive

◆ Grout in light blue or red

## Jewellery

Cut the tesserae into shape using a glass cutter or glass nibbling pincers. Make the edges round, as described on page 27. Then fix the tiles using silicone adhesive. For the red brooch, stick on aluminium foil beforehand, in order to give the transparent glass optimum reflection. The brooch can also be partially glued and the spaces in between filled with grout once the adhesive has dried.

## Tip

◆ You can also use the brooches as pendants. Fix a hook made from wire on the underneath side.

## Fish

ut out the fish shape using a saw
nd apply adhesive primer. Then
tick on the tesserae using a raised
dhesive bed (see page 82). First
ay the eye and then the open
mouth (using the red stones). Then
dd the dark blue border and a
wave-shaped line to divide off the
ead with an edge length of 5mm
³⁄₁₆in). Fill the surface in between.
tick on the fin and the individual
cales. Finally, create the tail fin,
irst the dark border and then the
ight blue surface. Create the
order, as described on page 82.

**MOTIF HEIGHT**
Approx. 25cm (10in)

**MATERIALS**

◆ MDF board, 1cm (³⁄₈in)
  thick, 50 x 20cm
  (20 x 8in)

◆ Smalti or glass mosaic
  pieces: 400 x blue
  shades, 30 x yellow, 85 x
  orange and 55 x red

◆ Cement-based tile
  adhesive in white

◆ Colour pigment in blue

◆ Jigsaw with a fine blade

◆ Sandpaper

◆ Adhesive primer

◆ 2 metal picture hooks,
  approx. 3cm (1¹⁄₈in) wide

**TEMPLATE**
Page 126

# DIRECT METHOD

**MOTIF SIZE**
Diameters approx. 22cm
(8¾in) and 28cm (11in)

**MATERIALS**

◆ Glass tesserae: blue,
  green and mother-of-
  pearl, 2cm (¾in) square,
  approx. 0.04m²
  (0.048yd²) per plate

◆ Stoneware tesserae in
  white, 2.3cm (¹⁵⁄₁₆in),
  approx. 0.06m² (0.07yd²)
  per plate

◆ Plates, sizes as above

◆ Shells, 3cm (1¹⁄₈in) long

◆ Adhesive primer

◆ Cement-based tile
  adhesive

◆ Grout in white

## Maritime plates

The plates are made using the
direct method, as described on
pages 32–33. Start gluing at the
centre of the spiral and continue
laying the tesserae in a spiral
towards the outside. Then lay the
border and finally fill in the
background.

## Tips

◆ The plates are good practise
for beginners. However, you will
need patience when cutting the
tesserae, but the design will let
you get away with minor errors.

◆ You can also use the large
plate as an underplate.

# 5 INDIRECT METHOD

## Basic equipment

The tools and materials needed for the indirect method are the same as those needed for the direct method (see page 28). You will also need to have the following to hand, as they will not appear in the list of materials:

- Mosaic glue, wood glue diluted with water or flour paste
- Flat paintbrush (for applying glue and dissolving)
- Copier paper or strong packing or drawing paper with the design drawn on it
- Washing-up liquid
- Permanent ink felt pens
- Toothed spatula for laying tiles (spreading glue)
- Tweezers
- Parcel tape, wood glue, wood saw, rechargeable screwdriver, wire cutters (for flat cast)
- Piece of wood the size of the mosaic (two for flat casts)

The indirect method, also known as the reverse technique, is one that has been used since the 13th century and is most frequently used by professionals today. Its advantage over the direct method is that the work can be comfortably done at home and put in its final position when it is completed. The design can also be divided up, so that several people can be working on one mosaic at the same time. The indirect method is especially suitable for working on table-top or flooring pieces, since for these you need to achieve an absolutely level surface, even when using different thicknesses of material.

A disadvantage of the indirect method is that the mosaic has to be worked on as a mirror image, and while laying it, you can only see the reverse side. This is why this method is only suitable for material that is dyed right through, with the same colour on both sides. In all other cases, the reciprocal method can be used, which is also described in this section (see page 42).

Indirect method – for level surfaces; easier working

38

# PAPER AND PASTE

The same tools and materials are used for the indirect method as are needed for the direct method (see page 28), plus also paper the size of the mosaic and water-soluble paste. This can be a diluted, water-soluble wood glue (ratio 1:1), a special mosaic glue or a hand-made flour paste. To make this, put a dessertspoonful of white flour into a saucepan and mix until smooth with 100ml (3½fl oz) water. Then boil the mixture until the desired consistency is reached, adding more water where necessary. After boiling, add five drops of gum arabic. This amount is enough for paper up to a size of 80cm (31½in) square. The flour paste will keep for up to a week in the fridge. Keep in a screw-top jar.

For small mosaics, normal drawing or copier paper is suitable as a temporary base (up to size A4/US letter, 80gsm); for larger work, you will need strong paper, such as packing or drawing paper (90gsm or 120gsm).

## EXPERT TIP

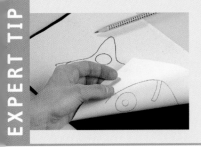

### Making templates less complicated
The template must be able to be viewed as a mirror image for the indirect method. It is easy to do if you simply trace your drawing onto the reverse side using carbon paper. To do this, place the carbon paper underneath with the coated side uppermost and draw over the lines. Attach the papers to one another so that they do not slip. The traced design can be used under the mosaic as a guideline (be careful with light stoneware mosaic; see third Tip on the right).

## Step-by-step instructions

### Stick the mosaic to paper

**1**
Stick the tesserae to the design using water-soluble adhesive (see above). Using a paintbrush, paint the adhesive on the flat, upper surface of the tessera or onto the corresponding area of the design and press the stone down lightly. The adhesive will dry after only a short time and the stone will be held securely. Continue in this way until the whole picture is laid.

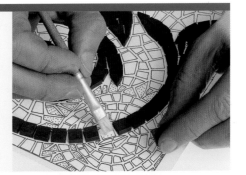

### Prepare the base

**2**
Paint very porous bases, such as wooden board, with an adhesive primer. This prevents moisture from being drawn too quickly into the base and improves adhesion (see also page 29).

## Tips & Tricks

◆ Rather than paper, cotton gauze (tarlatan) can also be used as a temporary base for the indirect method.

◆ When drawing your template for the indirect method, do not use water-soluble felt or coloured pens, as these could later come off on the mosaic.

◆ Take care when using carbon paper for tracing the template onto light stoneware (see page 13 and the Expert Tip on the left). It is better to trace the design on a layout table with a permanent ink pen or have a mirror-image copy made by a copy shop.

◆ Do not paint too large an area of paper with mosaic glue or other adhesive, otherwise the paper will become soggy. Only use as much glue as required, which will then make it easier to remove the paper later.

Indirect method continued

Indirect method
continued

## Tips & Tricks

◆ For a picture sized 20cm (8in) square, you will need around 30ml (1fl oz) water, into which you should stir the corresponding amount of tile adhesive or grout powder.

## Advice

◆ Make sure that there are no fragments between the stones and the paper. Keep wiping fragments off your design with a brush. This will result in the stones adhering well and also reduces the risk of injury.

◆ Do not confuse adhesive mortar with grouting compound. Even though both are cement-based, they have different adhesive strengths. Adhesive mortar is for sticking individual tesserae to the base; grouting compound is merely for filling the remaining gaps between the individual stones.

### Painting the base with adhesive

**3** Mix the tile adhesive as described on page 32, Step 3, and use it to paint an even layer 2mm ($^3/_{32}$in) thick onto the base. Apply with a trowel or spatula and spread with a toothed spatula used for laying tiles. Smooth out the grooves again, otherwise small tesserae will sink into it later. Work very carefully at the edges.

### Grouting the reverse

**4** Mix the grout without getting it too wet (see page 33, Step 6). Place the mosaic on a mobile wooden base or similar and apply the grout. Carefully press the mixture into the gaps using a trowel or a rubber board. Fill as many gaps as possible.

### Remove excess grout

**5** Remove excess grout by working diagonally, in the direction of the grout where possible, to prevent the grout from being pulled out again. The grout should just be between the gaps and not on the reverse of the tesserae. Work quickly, as the mosaic glue will begin to dissolve as soon as the damp grout penetrates the paper.

### Place the base on the mosaic

**6** Now lay the base with the sticky side exactly on the grouted reverse of the mosaic. Press firmly so that the adhesive layer sticks well to the mosaic. Place one hand under the wooden board on which the work lies, and with the other hand on top, press together and turn the mosaic over (sandwich procedure). Now the mosaic is the right way up.

### Press on the mosaic

**7** Press again from the top of the stones onto the adhesive bed, using a clean trowel or a piece of smooth wood onto the paper. Should any bubbles occur, burst them with a pointed object through the paper, so that the trapped air can escape.

## Hammer the mosaic flat

**8**

To ensure that the stones are all the same height, work on it again with a hammer and the trowel. Then leave to rest (about 15–30 minutes). Test how secure the tesserae are by trying to move a stone. If it moves easily, leave a little longer. The adhesive should not harden completely, otherwise you will be unable to correct any errors (see Step 11).

## Remove the paper

**9**

Paint the paper with water to remove it. To do this, heat some water and add a few drops of washing-up liquid. This will speed up and facilitate the removal of the paper. Then paint all over the paper using the paintbrush, several times, if necessary. The paper should be thoroughly wet through, but make sure that the water does not seep underneath at the edges.

## Pull off the paper

**10**

After a few minutes, the mosaic glue should have dissolved enough so that you can pull off the paper. Lift the paper carefully at the corner with tweezers and pull it back flat. The paper should be pulled off in one piece. If it is difficult to remove, wait a little longer and if necessary re-wet the paper.

## Remove mosaic glue and hammer flat

**11**

Wash off the remaining mosaic glue using a slightly damp sponge. Ensure that it does not become too wet and dissolve the grout again. Stones that look as though they are going to come out should be reset using tweezers. Use the trowel or a piece of wood to even out the surface again.

## Grout the front and clean

**12**

As grouting from the reverse can often mean that not all the holes are filled, grout the piece again from the front. Leave to dry out overnight. Mix the grouting compound a little thinner, so that small, open places are easier to fill. Spread, remove the excess and clean the mosaic (see page 33, Step 8).

## Tips & Tricks

◆ To exchange individual stones, remove them carefully with tweezers, as in Step 11. Before you set a new stone, using a small spatula, paint some adhesive into the hole, if necessary. Then insert the new stone and press it carefully with the trowel so that it is the same height as the other stones. Once you have made all your improvements to the mosaic, hammer the whole surface again with the trowel or a smooth piece of wood (it should be quite smooth) and wipe over with a sponge cloth.

◆ If you want to incorporate individual pieces (such as glass nuggets or shells) into an indirectly laid mosaic, you can do this by following Step 11.

◆ It is very likely that a cement film will appear again when drying. Do not attempt to wipe this away immediately. You will only wash cement out of the gaps (see under Advice on page 33).

## Advice

◆ Do not attempt to speed up the grout-drying process by using a hair-dryer on the picture or full sunshine. This will lead to cracks in the material.

◆ Clean all equipment immediately after use with water. Do not pour dirty water down the drain or the toilet. Pour it away in the garden, on a gravel path or down a street drain.

## Please note

Tile adhesive and grout contain cement and can irritate the eyes, respiratory system and the skin. This is why you should always wear protective clothing (gloves and dust mask). Should tile adhesive or grout come into contact with the eyes, rinse them out immediately with water and consult a doctor. If it comes into contact with skin, wash off immediately with lots of water. Children should not be allowed access to powder containing cement.

# RECIPROCAL TECHNIQUE

The indirect method is suitable only for materials that are dyed right through, such as glass mosaic or natural stone, and not for glazed ceramic pieces, where the reverse side is always of a different colour to the top. When laying the mosaic, you can no longer see the pattern and colour.

The reciprocal technique is suitable for different thicknesses of ceramic pieces that need to be laid on a level surface. It is a type of direct/indirect laying method. The tesserae are pressed into a layer of clay, plastic or lime and then paper or thin cotton is glued over it using water-soluble adhesive. Once the glue has dried, you will have a reverse-laid mosaic, which you can remove from the base on the paper or fabric and continue as described in the instructions (see page 39 onwards).

# WALL AND FLOOR ASSEMBLY

If you want to mount your picture on a fixed base, such as on the wall or on the floor, follow the step-by-step instructions on pages 39–40 up to Step 5. Then the mosaic picture, grouted from behind, is carefully lifted and pressed into the adhesive bed in the corresponding place. It is very important that you work quickly when doing this, so that the paper (it will have already become damp from applying the grout) does not tear (preferably use strong paper, about 120gsm). If your mosaic picture is larger than about 30cm (12in) square, it should not be mounted in one piece. The danger of the paper tearing is too great. You should therefore break it up into several pieces by cutting along the grouting using a sharp knife (cutter). Grout the individual pieces together to form the whole picture again in their final position. Before you make large-scale pieces, you should practise mounting indirectly laid mosaics on small pieces first.

# MAKING A FLAT CAST

The advantage of a flat cast is that the height of the material does not matter, as it will be laid in a thick layer of cement. Hand-cut natural stone is mainly used for this technique. The base is also frost-proof, which means that pieces for the garden or a table top can be made using the flat cast. However, there is one drawback: the mosaic is very heavy. If you want to work on a mosaic picture to decorate a wall using this technique, you should place it in a metal frame (see page 34) with a fixing hook.

(see page 34)

## Advice

◆ Flat casts can also be made using the direct method, similar to the thick-bed procedure used when laying tiles. The advantage is that, due to the thick bed of mortar, various other thick materials can be laid level. Mix the mortar using equal parts dry cement and sand and add one part lime with a trowel. Add water and mix well with the modeller's spatula until you have a soft, fine mixture. Only work with as much mortar as you can use within around 2 hours.

◆ Spray the base with water first. Apply the mixture (depending on the thickness of the material) about 1.5cm (⅝in) thick and create a firm, compact bed for gluing.

◆ Then transfer the template and lay the stones, preferably one stone at a time. You will be able to push the stones most easily into the bed of mortar when they are wedge-shaped underneath.

## Step-by-step instructions

### Putting together a wooden frame

**1** Make a frame from planks of wood in the desired height and size of the flat cast. Screw the wood together at the corners (do not nail, as the planks must be taken apart again). To ensure that the mosaic board does not stick to the wooden frame, you can smear the wood with petroleum jelly or stick parcel tape on it.

### Cover the base

**2** Cut a piece of wood the size of the frame and cover it with plastic film. Then place the wooden frame onto the board of the same size and tape them both together with parcel tape.

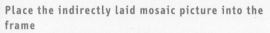

### Place the indirectly laid mosaic picture into the frame

**3** Place the indirectly laid mosaic (see the step-by-step instructions on pages 39–40 up to Step 5) into the frame with the paper side down. Cut the paper first to the right size; it must not be too big.

(see the step-by-step instructions on pages 39–40 up to Step 5)

Making a flat cast continued

Making a flat cast
continued

## Tips & Tricks

After compressing again in all directions using a long plank of wood (Step 7), finally smooth off your work using the trowel. The trowel smoothes the surface but without compacting at all.

◆ A flat cast should be as thin as possible, as it can become very heavy. Bear this in mind when selecting the wood for the frame, since it must all be filled. For the thickness of the cast, as a rule of thumb, the larger the cast, the thicker the bed of mortar; it should be at least 2cm (¾in) thick.

### Grout the mosaic from the reverse

**4**

Now grout the mosaic with sand and cement from the reverse side using a round brush (mix two to three parts sand and one part cement with water to make a really thin mixture). Press the mixture into the gaps well; do not spread, as this could cause the stones to slip. Just press into the gaps and clean the area around the mosaic.

### Half-fill the frame with mortar

**5**

Half-fill the frame with a crumbly mortar mixture that is not too damp (ready-mix trass cement/mortar or a mixture of one part cement and three parts sand). Press the mixture in well and stamp flat with a piece of wood so that there are no holes.

### Insert wire frame

**6**

Now, using wire cutters, cut out a wire frame that is a little smaller than the frame and lay this on the bed of mortar. This wire insert makes the mosaic base more secure. Press the wire frame down well. To prevent the netting curling up at the corners, place some thick balls of mortar on top. These are pressed flat in Step 7.

### Completely fill the frame with mortar

**7**

Now fill the whole frame with mortar. Compact the mixture well again by stamping flat with a piece of wood first, then smoothing out again using a long plank of wood and finally smoothing with the trowel (see Tip top left). There should be no holes in the mortar layer. Take your time with this.

### Cover and turn the mosaic

**8**

Place plastic sheeting over the mortar bed and a board on top. Now leave the work to rest for two hours. Stick everything together with parcel tape and turn over like a sandwich. Then remove the board, which is now on top.

### Remove the paper

Soften the paper with hot water and a few drops of washing-up liquid to dissolve the water-soluble mosaic glue. Use a paintbrush to moisten the paper until it can be peeled away. Peel back the paper as flat as possible to avoid ripping any stones out of the mortar.

## 9

### Wash off the mosaic glue

Now wash off the mosaic glue from the surface. Then wipe over the mortar again with a clean sponge to make the surface smooth. If the mortar has not yet set, wait a little longer. The stones should not move any more.

## 10

### Hammer the mosaic flat

Using a hammer and trowel, hammer the mosaic flat, including the background layer. Wipe all over with a damp sponge and polish the stones with a sponge cloth. Mortar will always come out of the gaps when you go over it with the trowel. Leave to dry covered with sheeting and a wooden board.

## 11

### Grout the mosaic from the front

Depending on the mosaic picture, decide whether to grout it from the front too. Mix a thin grouting compound (see Step 4) and press into the gaps with a round brush. Clean once more.

## 12

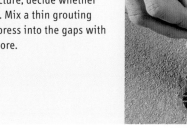

### Remove the frame

After two to three days, you can carefully remove the wooden frame. However, the mortar will still not be fully set. Leave the mosaic board to rest for a few more days.

## 13

## Tips & Tricks

◆ Washing off mosaic glue takes longer with natural stone than it does with glass or ceramic tesserae. Wipe just over the mosaic and not over the mortar layer, otherwise the colour can change due to being mixed with the leftover glue.

◆ In the case of some materials, cement will lodge in the pores and cannot be washed away with water. This can be removed with citric acid (remember to wear gloves!). Take care with natural stone, polished surfaces in particular: test the reaction first in an inconspicuous place. Dab on the acid with a sponge and briefly allow it to react, then rub the surface with a brush. Wash off with plenty of water.

◆ As natural stone loses its intensity of colour, treat it with stone oil afterwards. Apply with a cloth or brush and dab off the excess oil with a rag. Never use clear varnish!

## Face

Make a frame 40 x 29.5cm (15¾ x 11¾in) (inner dimensions) by sawing two pieces each of tile batten in 50cm (19¾in) and 39.5cm (15½in) lengths. Stick some parcel tape around the edge. Make the reverse (indirect method) mosaic (see page 38 onwards) in natural stone (cut into pieces using a hammer and awl, see page 26) as a flat cast (see pages 43–45).

## Tip

◆  Working with natural stone, especially breaking it up with a hammer and awl, requires practise. Beginners would be better making the face from stoneware.

**MOTIF HEIGHT**
Approx. 40cm (15¾in)

**MATERIALS**

◆  Marble rods or marble cubes in bright colours, approx. 1.5kg (3lb 5oz)

◆  Trass cement/mortar, grain size 0–4mm (0–5/32in)

◆  800ml (1½ pints) water

◆  Tile batten, 2.5 x 5cm (1 x 2in), 2m (2¼yd) long

◆  2 plastic sheets, 50 x 39.5cm (19¾ x 15½in)

◆  Aviary wire approx. 39 x 28.5cm (15¼ x 11¼in)

4 wood screws, 8cm (3in) long

**TEMPLATE**
Page 126

# PROJECTS

## Table with fish

**MOTIF SIZE**
Diameter approx. 60cm (23¾in)

**MATERIALS**

◆  Concrete base, 3cm (1⅛in) thick, 59cm (23¼in) diameter

◆  Glass mosaic stones: 400 x white, approx. 40 x dark red, approx. 15 each x bright red and salmon, plus approx. 5 each x rust brown and black, 2.5cm (1in) square

◆  Iridescent glass tesserae in black (eye), 2.5cm (1in) square

◆  Two-component adhesive

◆  Grout in silver grey

**TEMPLATE**
Page 127

For the fish, cut out strips about 4mm (5/32in) wide, 1.2cm (½in) long, squares 5mm (3/16in) and irregular pieces, plus about 60 white squares, as well as round and conical shapes (for the eyes). Lay using the indirect method. First the eye: the round piece and conical pieces around it, then red and white stones and finally diagonally laid brown strips. Next lay the body: mouth, body contours and tail fin with strips, and then the inner area with squares and triangles. Finally, lay the fins (lengthways strips and squares above, elsewhere just strips) and the barbels. For the background, lay white strips, and squares in shades of red in the *Opus Vermiculatum* (page 14). Edge the mosaic with quartered stones and stick halved stones around the edge of the table. Finish laying the mosaic and then grout.

## Dolphin

The mosaic is made using the
indirect method (see page 38
onwards). Glue the pieces of wood
around the base (see page 34)
before laying the stones (see page
– the spiral is laid from the
centre outwards). To make the
white background tiles stand out,
grout the mosaic in grey.

## Tip

The mosaic can be used either
as a coaster or a small picture. The
motif is very good for practising
cutting mosaic materials and the
level of work is quite manageable.

### MOTIF SIZE
20cm (8in) square

### MATERIALS

◆ Glass mosaic in white,
three shades of green
and two shades of blue,
2cm (¾in) square, in
total approx. 0.04m²
(0.048yd²), 500g (1lb 2oz)

◆ MDF board, 20cm (8in)
square, 1cm (⅜in) thick

◆ Pieces of wood, 2cm x
5mm (¾ x ³⁄₁₆in), 85cm
(33½in) long

◆ Grey cement-based tile
adhesive

◆ Grey grouting compound

◆ Adhesive primer

◆ Wood glue

### TEMPLATE
Page 127

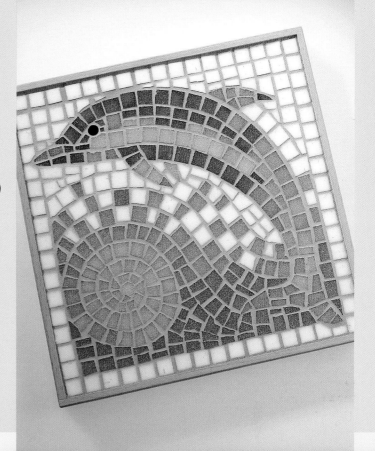

# INDIRECT METHOD

### MOTIF HEIGHT
Approx. 40cm (15¾in)

### MATERIALS

◆ Marble rods or marble
cubes in bright colours,
approx. 2.5kg (5lb 8oz)

◆ Trass cement/mortar,
grain size 0–4mm
(0–⁵⁄₃₂in)

◆ 800ml (1½ pints) water

◆ Tile batten, 2.5 x 5cm (1 x
2in), 2m (2¼yd) long

◆ 2 plastic sheets, 50 x
39.5cm (19¾ x 15½in)

◆ Aviary wire approx. 39 x
28.5cm (15¼ x 11¼in)

◆ 4 wood screws, 8cm (3in)
long

### TEMPLATE
Page 126

## Bird

Make a frame 40 x 29.5cm (15¾ x
11¾in) (inner dimensions),
sawing two pieces each of tile
batten in 50cm (19¾in) and
39.5cm (15½in) lengths. Stick
parcel tape around the edge.
Make the reverse mosaic as a flat
cast (see instructions for the Face
above opposite).

## Tip

◆ You will find another bird
motif on page 118.

# 6 MOSAIC OBJECTS

## Basic equipment

When making three-dimensional objects, you will need the same basic equipment as for the direct method (see page 28). Have these items to hand, as they will not be specified in the list of materials.

Covering an object with mosaic is one of the oldest techniques of the art of mosaics. This approach was widely used, especially by the ancient civilizations of America. The Mayas and Aztecs were skilful at decorating everyday objects, wooden masks and human skulls. Small objects covered in mosaic were also produced in Peru. Materials such as gold, pieces of bone, shells, ivory and semi-precious stones were used. In Ancient Greece and Italy, mosaics were mainly laid flat on walls and floors. In Europe, it was some time later before they were laid as three-dimensional objects, from the Art Nouveau period onwards. Gaudí was the pioneer in this method and was followed by many artisans, making Barcelona an ideal place for viewing mosaic objects. Whole houses in the style of the turn of the 20th century and even churches like La Sagrada Familia were covered with thousands of mosaic pieces. Niki de Saint Phalle's Tarot garden near Garavicchio (north of Rome) is also worth a visit.

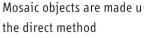

Mosaic objects are made u
the direct method

# CHOICE OF OBJECT and MATERIALS

## Suitable objects

It does not matter if the basic object is old and ugly, as it will no longer be visible under the mosaic work. You should pay close attention to the shape of the object. As a rule of thumb, the simpler and clearer the object, the more suitable it is. An ornate, filigree picture frame would not be suitable, whereas a simple, wide-edged wooden frame would make a wonderful surface for covering. Also avoid strong curves, as the mosaic pieces need to be very small in order for the mosaic to work.

However, even though the object to be covered can be old, it must still be stable. A scratch, dent or split edge does not matter. However, a wooden frame with a wobbly corner is not suitable. The mosaic layer is only a covering and does not provide stability and may itself crack after a while. This is why it is important to take your time and stabilize the object found, where needed.

## Suitable materials

As three-dimensional mosaic objects often do not need a smooth surface, as for example with mosaic flooring, virtually any material in any thickness and shape can be used. There is also no need to worry about it being frostproof, since the work is intended for indoor use, giving you an unlimited choice of materials, which can easily become daunting. So make sure that you do not end up with an unmanageable pile of materials!

Apart from the traditional mosaic materials, such as glass, stoneware, tile or marble, you can also use broken crockery, found objects from the beach (mainly broken, polished glass bottles or tiles), glass marbles and nuggets, shells, buttons, gravel and much more. A prerequisite for success in this area is a real passion for collecting.

## Advice

◆ Look for objects to stick mosaics on that have simple shapes, such as pots, vases, picture frames, ceramic objects, spheres, dishes and so on.

49

# Make your own 3-D EFFECTS

## Tips & Tricks

◆ Styrodur® sheets can be stepped and stuck together (with cement-based tile adhesive). The edges are then painted with tile adhesive mixed with 30 per cent quartz sand and rounded off. This gives a 3-D-effect base, which is good for covering.

## Advice

◆ A Styrodur® sheet consists of pressed and shaped polystyrol foam and is coated on both sides with glass fibre and special mortar. Thin sheets can be cut with a cutter; for thicker sheets or round shapes, use a jigsaw. You can buy Styrodur® sheets from DIY stores.

You can easily make your own 3-D bases. Round and square wooden planks are good for this, as well as PU foam, Styrodur® sheets, Styropor® shapes, wire frames and concrete.

**Wooden planks** can be stuck to the base to good effect and then covered with tesserae, together with the rest of the surface. Do not use overly small wooden planks, otherwise you will have to cut the pieces of material into tiny shapes.

You can make relief structures using **PU foam**. It comes in aerosol cans and can be used to create any shape. Once it has dried (this takes about 24 hours), the stiff foam can be cut into shape using a cutter. Then paint adhesive primer onto the material (PU foam expands considerably). Once the aerosol has been opened, it is best to use it all, as the rest will easily dry out.

**Styrodur® sheets** are very light and so add very little to the weight of the mosaic (see Advice below left). They are fixed to the base using tile adhesive; they can also be used as the base for pictures or table tops. Any kind of shape can be cut from the sheet using a cutter or, for thicker or round pieces, a jigsaw.

A large selection of **Styropor® shapes** are available from craft shops. They can be cut using a sharp knife and stuck to the base. Make sure that you use a special Styropor® adhesive, as most normal adhesives would destroy the material. A flexible tile adhesive is suitable for use when covering with mosaic.

You can make your own sculptures using a **fine wire netting**. Tie the wire pieces together using wire on a roll and wrap with plaster-of-Paris bandages (for indoor use only). This prevents the tesserae from slipping through the netting.

You can also make the basic framework for mosaic objects yourself from **concrete**. They work well with ferrous cement that contains iron. First make the basic framework from bending construction steel and, where necessary, welding it together. Individual pieces can be secured using wire. This basic framework is then covered with fine wire netting (aviary wire, cut into long pieces) and secured with wire. For larger objects, fill the hole in the centre with paper, Styropor® or other lightweight material.

Now apply several layers of lime cement or trass cement/mortar, mix a thick mixture of about 1kg (2lb 4oz) dry mixture and 170ml (6fl oz) water. Then apply to the sculpture, pressing with one hand behind against the netting, while applying the mortar with the other hand. Build up several thin layers and allow to dry in between. If you break off work for longer, then the dried layer of mortar should be dampened again first. This work takes a lot of time and the sculpture becomes very heavy (if necessary, construct in situ).

## Step-by-step instructions

### 1 Prepare the base

Prepare the base as described on page 29. If a pattern has to be created, transfer the design using carbon paper. The pattern should not be overly complicated, especially if you are a beginner, since when the soft, opaque adhesive is applied (see page 32, Step 3), it is usually hidden.

### 2 Cover with stones, piece by piece

Apply the adhesive about 2mm (³⁄₃₂in) thick using a spatula or modeller's spatula and press in the cut mosaic pieces (see page 20 onwards). To achieve an even surface on the sphere, press carefully. Leave a gap of at least 1mm (¹⁄₃₂in) (the adhesive should not seep over the top of the stone). Leave the work to dry overnight.

### 3 Mix the grouting compound and apply

Mix the grouting compound (see page 33, Step 6). Press the grouting compound into the gaps all over the sphere using a round brush or a small sponge. Spread the grout several times in various directions over the whole mosaic. You can also do this by hand wearing thick rubber gloves.

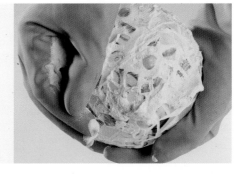

### 4 Wipe off the excess grouting compound

When all the gaps are filled, wipe off the excess grout with a sponge. But first allow the grout to set briefly, as otherwise you will wipe too much grout out of the gaps. Take care not to work with a sponge that is too wet (see also page 33, Steps 8 and 9).

### 5 Finish off the mosaic

Do not try to make your mosaic absolutely clean immediately after grouting. Leave it to rest until the grout begins to dry (10–30 minutes, depending on the temperature and humidity). Then you can rub off the remaining marks from the surface using a dry cloth (see also page 33, Step 10).

## Advice

◆ For objects covered with transparent glass, such as lanterns or vases, silicone adhesive is the glue to use (see also page 30).

◆ Make sure that the surface of the tesserae is not covered with adhesive. Wipe off any soiling immediately with a damp sponge.

## Tips & Tricks

◆ Instead of spreading the base with adhesive, each individual mosaic piece can be covered on the reverse. This method takes longer, but it does mean that the pattern drawn on the object is not covered with adhesive.

◆ Only cover one side of a sphere first and then, after drying, turn and cover the other side (see also Garden Sphere on page 91, Step 5).

## Dish

Colour the adhesive powder blue (see page 57, Step 2) and apply an approximately 4mm (5/32in) thick circle in the centre of the dish. Lay the tesserae from the centre of the dish using the direct method, but with a raised adhesive bed (see Decorative Plate on page 66, Step 3). Use tweezers to place the stones. Allow the light blue mortar to dry and then prepare the red adhesive compound. Apply this almost to the edge of the dish and lay the mosaic pieces. Finally, apply blue mortar again and cover with mirrored and glass stones. Leave at least overnight to dry.

**MOTIF SIZE**
Diameter 30cm (12in)

**MATERIALS**

◆ Wooden dish, diameter 30cm (12in)

◆ Tiffany glass stones: 55 x red, 33 x orange, 45 x yellow, 27 x green, 50 x blue and 9 x light blue, 1cm (3/8in) square to 1 x 2cm (3/8 x 3/4in)

◆ 27 mirrored stones, 1cm (3/8in) square

◆ 66 millefiori discs in matching colours, 7–8mm (5/16in) diameter

◆ Cement-based tile adhesive in white

◆ Colour pigment in blue and red

# PROJECTS

**MOTIF HEIGHT**
Approx. 17cm (6¾in)

**MATERIALS**

◆ Ceramic figure, approx. 16cm (6¼in) high

◆ Cement-based tile adhesive

◆ Grouting compound in grey (frostproof if used outdoors)

◆ 2 glass eyes, diameter 8mm (5/16in)

◆ Approx. 120 stoneware tesserae in black and white, 2.3cm (15/16in) square

## Two cats

Prime the ceramic figures with adhesive primer and leave to dry. Cut the stoneware tesserae into about 1cm (3/8in) square irregular pieces and stick onto the bodies of the cats using the direct method (see page 28 onwards). In this case, the original model already has whiskers that can be included in the mosaic. Otherwise, you could stick on broom bristles, for example. Work piece by piece and leave to dry for 24 hours. Grout with grey grouting compound and then clean.

## China sphere

he china sphere is made as
escribed in the step-by-step
nstructions on page 51.

## Tip

he china spheres will always look
ifferent, depending on the design
f crockery used. You will find a
urther example on page 73.

**MOTIF HEIGHT**
Approx. 13cm (5in)

**MATERIALS**

- China sphere, diameter
  approx. 13cm (5in)
- Cement-based tile
  adhesive
- Grouting compound in
  white
- Old crockery
- Glass nuggets in green,
  diameter 2cm (¾in)

# MOSAIC OBJECTS

**MOTIF HEIGHT**
Approx 52cm (20in)

**MATERIALS**

- Floor-standing vase,
  diameter 46cm (18in),
  52cm (20½in) high
- 5 marble tiles in white,
  4.5cm (1¾in) square
- Approx. 20 floor tiles in
  black, grey, beige and
  light green
- Approx. 10 stoneware
  tiles in gold, 10cm (4in)
  square
- Approx. 35 flat pebbles
- Cement-based tile
  adhesive
- Wide grouting compound
  in grey

**TEMPLATE**
Page 127

## Floor-standing vase

Divide the white marble tiles
diagonally using the tile cutter
and cut into 16 triangular pieces
(see page 25). Stick around the
opening of the vase in a star
shape. Break the floor tiles into
small pieces with a hammer.
Cover the centre of the circle with
pebbles, then lay a 5cm (2in) wide
ring of fragments and around this
lay a ring about 2cm (2in) wide.
Stick gold fragments onto the
sweeping scroll. Stick roughly 15
rectangles around the base, about
6 x 11cm (2⅜ x 4¼in). Fill in the
rest of the surface with long or
square pieces about 10 x 15cm (4
x 6in).

# LIVING ROOM ACCESSORIES

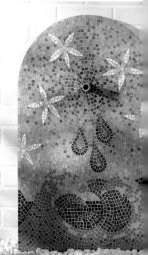

## IDEAS FOR OUTDOORS

# MOSAIC ART

# PROJECTS

## Lots of great ideas

In this Projects section, the largest, practical part of the book, you will find over 80 ideas for around the home and for a beautiful exterior, as well as for mosaic art in the Ancient Roman style and, in a more modern style, pieces that are bright and colourful or sophisticated and simple. The ideas include large and small ornamental items, such as dishes, candleholders, lanterns, spheres, mirror frames, stools, table tops and much more. The detailed instructions mean that you can easily reproduce them or use them as inspiration for your own projects.

## Practical shopping lists

Every mosaic is accompanied by a list of materials required. Everything you need for the project is listed, apart from the basic equipment itemized in the workshop. You will also be told in the list of materials how big the original mosaic work is, and when a template is needed, you will be referred to the relevant page at the back of the book (see Templates section, pages 126–130).

## Tips and tricks for success

As in the workshop, you will find numerous Tips and Tricks in the Projects section. These can be clever 'tricks' to make it easier to reproduce the object, practical advice on what to do when something goes wrong or inventive tips for an alternative or further application. Often included are additional step-by-step explanatory photos or helpful details.

## Advice

◆ The knowledge gained in the workshop is a prerequisite for reproducing these mosaic items and is not described in detail again. However, you can quickly read back over the technique using the reference to the relevant workshop page, if you find that you have forgotten any stage of the process.

◆ The list of materials for each project does not list again the basic tools and materials given in the workshop.

◆ The items in the Projects section are divided into levels of difficulty, as follows:

◐         simple
◐◐      a little more difficult
◐◐◐  advanced

# LIVING ROOM
# ACCESSORIES

# MILLEFIORI FRAMES

**1.** Remove the pane of glass from the picture frame. Sand the wooden surface and stain the side edges using a thin brush. Dilute the stain slightly with water. Paint adhesive primer onto the front of the frame.

**2** Mix some adhesive powder with coloured pigment. Only add a very little pigment to achieve the desired blend. Add water and mix to form a soft compound. Then apply 3–4mm (⅛in) thick to the frame with a small spatula. Wear protective gloves when working.

**3a** For the blue frame, press the millefiori discs into the damp base compound using tweezers. First of all, lay the pieces around the outer edge, then place those around the inner edge.

**3b** For the red frame, cut the glass tesserae into triangles and strips (see pages 24 and 26). It is advisable to cut out the shapes before mixing the adhesive using the glass nibbling pincers or the glass cutter. Press in the millefiori discs; cut some of them in half first using the mosaic pincers. Use tweezers to lay them. Start with the four corners and stick the mosaic pieces in a star formation around each disc. Make sure that you vary the colours and shapes as much as possible.

**3c** For the green frame, press the millefiori discs into the adhesive compound with tweezers. First lay the discs in the four corners, then lay the others at different heights in between. In the corners, around the millefiori discs, press in glass rods vertically and link to the other discs with wavy lines of rocaille beads. Use tweezers to pick up and press in the beads.

**4** Leave the frame to dry for around 24 hours and then replace the pane of glass.

## LEVEL OF DIFFICULTY
◔

## MOTIF HEIGHTS
Blue frame approx. 13cm (5in)

Red and green frames approx. 16cm (6¼in)

## MATERIALS
- Wooden picture frame, 13 x 18cm (5 x 7in) or 16 x 21cm (6¼ x 8¼in)
- Tile adhesive in white
- Colour pigment in blue, red or green
- Water-based wood stain in blue, red or green
- 24 millefiori discs in yellow, diameter 7mm (5/16in) (blue frame)
- 16 colourful millefiori discs, diameter 7mm–1cm (5/16–⅜in), and some glass tesserae in red, orange and yellow, 2cm (¾in) square (red frame)
- 14 colourful millefiori discs, diameter 1cm (⅜in), as well as rocaille and bar beads in shades of green (for the green frame)
- Sandpaper

## Tips & Tricks
- Make sure that you press all the pieces into the adhesive compound well, especially the little beads for the green frame, otherwise they will fall off after drying. Should this happen, they can be re-glued with a little adhesive and set again.

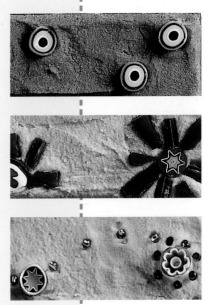

# DECORATIVE PASTELS

## Tips & Tricks

◆ Cover just half the sphere first, then turn it around and finish the other half.

◆ Place the sphere in a little dish so that you will be able to work on it more easily.

**LEVEL OF DIFFICULTY**
◐◐

**MOTIF SIZES**
Dish diameter approx. 32cm (12½in)

Sphere diameter approx. 13cm (5in)

**MATERIALS FOR DISH**

◆ Metal dish, diameter 31.5cm (12½in)

◆ Glass tesserae: 15 x yellow, 20 x pale pink, 30 x light blue, 35 x light green, 40 x green, plus 85 each x pale yellow and mid-green, 1.5cm (⅝in) square

◆ Silicone adhesive

◆ Grouting compound in light blue

◆ Adhesive primer

**DECORATIVE SPHERES**

◆ 2 ceramic spheres, diameter 12.5cm (5in)

◆ Glass tesserae in 12 x yellow, 50 x light green, 90 x light blue, 48 x pale pink (front sphere); 30 x light green, mid-green, whitish-green, pale pink and light blue, 40 x pale green and 10 x pale yellow (back sphere), 1.5cm (⅝in) square

◆ Silicone adhesive

◆ Grouting compound in light blue

**TEMPLATE**
Page 128

## Dish

1 Prime the metal dish with adhesive primer (see page 29), and when it has dried, transfer the motif onto it.

2 First of all, cut and stick on the small, round pieces. Cut the tesserae to the right shape (see page 27) and then divide the discs into four pieces, leaving five discs as they are (see template for sizes).

3 Then cut the green and five pale yellow stones into a conical shape (see page 26). Cut the remaining stones in half, according to the template; depending on the length, cut into quarters or halves and divide each of the two strips into four pieces (see page 80, bottom left photo).

4 Apply an even layer of silicone adhesive with the spatula 1mm (1/32 in) thick and stick on the circles as in the picture. First work circle by circle around the round centres (the direct method, see page 32 onwards).

5 Then create the background, working from the centre outwards and laying an even border around the edge. Some of the pieces have to be cut at a slant where the background meets the circle motif. Leave to dry overnight and then grout in light blue and finally clean thoroughly.

## Decorative spheres

1 Cover the sphere in the front starting at the centre point at the top. Lay a round, pale pink tessera (see page 27) and then a row of light green strips cut into thirds. Add a further row with 5 x 7.5mm (3/16 x 5/16 in) light blue stones. Finally, lay pale pink

strips cut into four lengthways. Then make the semicircular-shaped motif: pale yellow semicircle, with light blue stones cut into thirds and placed around it in a star shape, and pale pink conical pieces (see page 26). Fill the remaining area with small triangles that have edge lengths of 5mm (3/16in). Underneath, lay a row of light green strips cut into quarters and a further one of light blue stones cut in half. Cover the other half in the reverse order.

2 For the sphere at the back, cut out eight light blue, two whitish-green and a mid-green circle (see page 27), and arrange on the sphere, fixing with silicone adhesive. Then draw circles around three of them measuring 4.5cm (1¾in), 6.5cm (2½in) and 7.5cm (3in) in diameter and fill with tesserae. The pattern is inspired by the dish; in the front (visible circle), light blue stones, 5mm(3/16in) square and pale green stones cut into thirds are laid around the centre point. Continue working on the sphere at the top: lay a circle 1.5cm (⅝in) in diameter) from seven light green, long triangles and around them light blue squares, 5mm (3/16in), pale green and pale yellow strips, 5 x 7.5mm (3/16 x 5/16in), as well as a ring of mid-green strips cut into thirds. Place more light green, 5 x 7.5mm (3/16 x 5/16in) and pale pink strips cut into thirds, mid-green strips cut in half, light blue squares, 5mm (3/16in), halved whitish-green strips and pale green strips cut into thirds, mid-green squares, 5mm (3/16in), halved pale green strips and pale pink strips cut into thirds. Some of the stones have to be cut on a slant where they meet the circles.

3 Grout everything in light blue (see page 51) and clean after drying.

# CANDLEHOLDER

## Tips & Tricks

◆ You can obtain metal candleholders from craft or florist shops. The size of the drill bit (see Step 1) depends on the size of the spike of the candleholder.

◆ Stick the pieces of mirror so that they are not all evenly level, which will give a prettier light reflection.

## Advice

◆ Remember never to leave a burning candle unattended.

**LEVEL OF DIFFICULTY**
👁👁

**MOTIF HEIGHT**
Approx. 44cm (17¼in)

**MATERIALS**
- MDF board, 1cm (⅜in) thick, 45 x 20cm (17¾ x 8in)
- MDF board, 2cm (¾in) thick, 10cm (4in) square
- Metal candleholder with spike
- Mirrored glass, approx. 15cm (6in) square
- Approx. 36 glass tesserae in shades of green, 2cm (¾in) square
- Approx. 50 glass tesserae in shades of blue, 2cm (¾in) square
- Approx. 35 glass tesserae in black, 2cm (¾in) square
- Approx. 35 gold tesserae, 1cm (⅜in) square
- Cement-based tile adhesive or dispersion adhesive in white
- Grouting compound in white
- Adhesive primer
- Acrylic paint in turquoise
- Jigsaw with fine blade or electric fretsaw
- Sandpaper
- Jigsaw with fine blade or electric fretsaw
- Picture hooks, 2cm (¾in) wide

**TEMPLATE**
Page 127

1 Saw the oriental shape from the thick MDF board using a jigsaw and smooth the edges with sandpaper. Attach a picture hook to the reverse for hanging. Drill a hole in the middle of the small MDF board for the candleholder.

2 Glue the two MDF boards together with wood glue, then fix together with a screw clamp. Leave to dry for at least 24 hours. Finally, paint the lower decorative pieces and the top and bottom of the small MDF board in turquoise. Leave to dry.

3 Prime all the other pieces of wood with adhesive primer and leave to dry (see page 29). Transfer the design onto the piece of wood using carbon paper.

4 Cut about 125 pieces from the black glass mosaic stones and about 54 pieces from the mirrored glass 1cm (⅜in) square (using glass nibbling pincers or a glass cutter, see page 20 onwards).

5 The candleholder is made using the direct method (see page 28 onwards). Lay the borders using the black and the gold tesserae. Apply the adhesive about 1mm (1/32in) thick at the relevant places and press on the tesserae spaced about 1mm (1/32in) from one another. When sticking the tesserae around the edge, use a piece of wood as a guide to prevent the stones from jutting over the edge.

6 Cut out the green and blue tesserae in polygons, that is, in irregular shapes (see small photo below left), and stick on. Always work from the edge to the middle: first place pieces around the black and gold rows and then fill the area in between.

7 Cut more polygon pieces from the remaining mirrored glass and stick on.

8 Finally, stick the square, mirrored pieces onto the edge of the horizontal board. Leave to dry for 24 hours. Then grout with white grouting compound and clean after drying (see page 33).

# GLASS LAMPSHADES

## Tips & Tricks

◆ To make the glass lampshades, saw up glass bottles using a bucksaw with a ceramic or glass blade and then insert the light fitting. You could also simply buy glass lampshades and stick mosaics onto them. Do not choose traditional tesserae, as they will not let the light through.

**LEVEL OF DIFFICULTY**
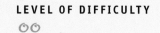

**MOTIF HEIGHT**
Approx. 12–18cm (4¾ x 7in)

**MATERIALS**

◆ Cut-off bottles, diameter 7cm (2¾in), 18cm (7in) high (yellow lampshade), diameter 9cm (3½in), 12cm (4¾in) high (red lampshade) or diameter 6.5cm (2½in), 14cm (5½in) high (green lampshade and nugget lampshade)

◆ 4 glass nuggets each in pale yellow and yellow, diameter 3cm (1⅛ in), and glass leftovers in shades of yellow (clear and milky), in total approx. 20 x 30cm (8 x 12in) (yellow lampshade)

◆ 14 glass nuggets in red, diameter 1.5cm (⅝in), and glass leftovers in shades of red, pink and orange (milky and transparent), in total approx. 15 x 30cm (6 x 12in) (red lampshade)

◆ Glass leftovers in various shades of green (clear and milky), in total approx 25 x 15cm (10 x 6in) (green lampshade)

◆ Approx. 150 glass nuggets in various transparent colours, 1.5–2cm (⅝–¾in) diameter (nugget lampshade)

◆ Silicone adhesive

◆ Grouting compound in yellow, red or green

**1** Cut the pieces of glass with the glass cutter or the glass nibbling pincers into various different-sized pieces: squares, triangles, strips and irregular shapes (see page 24 onwards). They are stuck to the base using silicone adhesive using the direct method (see page 51). Always apply the adhesive to one place at a time, only covering a surface that can be laid in around 10–15 minutes, and spread even using the spatula 1mm (1/32in) thick. Press the glass pieces in well so that there are no bubbles in between the two layers of glass.

**2a** For the yellow lampshade, stick on the glass nuggets first and then place the pale yellow, semicircular glass shapes below around the edge of the lampshade. Fill the remainder of the surface with mixed shades of yellow, leaving a slightly bigger gap between the semicircles and the background area.

**2b** For the red lampshade, stick the pattern on starting at the bottom edge of the lampshade: a row of strips, the glass nuggets and another row of strips in dark shades, continuing with squares and two rows of triangles, as well as horizontal strips in various shades. Fill the rest of the lampshade with triangular shapes.

**2c** Cover the green lampshade in the same way, starting at the bottom edge. For this one, the distances between the glass pieces are larger and are filled with grout after the adhesive has dried.

**2d** For the nugget lampshade, cover the upper and lower edges and then fill the surface in between. Put a pea-sized amount of silicone adhesive under each glass nugget and press in well. Then grout in beige.

**3** Leave the lampshades to dry overnight and then grout in the appropriate colour. After 24 hours, rinse with diluted vinegar and leave to dry. The acid will remove the dust left over from grouting (important with glass). Finally, insert the light fitting with bulb.

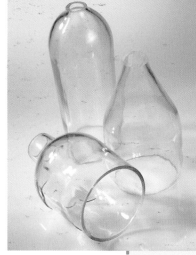

# GLASS VASES

...t out the pattern template and ...cure inside the vase with adhesive ...pe. The vases are covered using the ...rect method (see page 51). Score ...m (³⁄₈in) wide strips on the glass ...ith the glass cutter and snap using ...e breaking pincers (see page 24).

## ...ront vase

For this vase, nip half of the lilac ...ass into irregular triangles using ...e mosaic nippers; nip the other half ...to 5mm (³⁄₁₆in) wide strips and then ...alve these into squares. Also cut the ...bbed, old-rose-coloured glass into ...quares and the clear glass into irre- ...ular triangles.

Stick on the glass nuggets, ...ressing in well. Then apply silicone ...dhesive and spread evenly 1mm ...⁄₃₂in) thick using a spatula. Work ...iece by piece, one petal at a time. ...ress the glass pieces in well so that ...ere are no bubbles between the two ...yers of glass. The silicone adhesive ...hould not spill over onto the other ...reas. Stick the glass pieces very ...lose to one another; the smaller the ...aps in between, the better.

Edge the glass nuggets with two ...ows of square shapes and lay the ...uter three rows (pale lilac, ribbed ...ld rose and clear old rose), as well as ...he upper edge (checked pattern). Fill ...he area in between with irregular, ...ale lilac triangular shapes. Work in ...his way for all the petals; they are ...onnected together at the side. Then ...tick on the lower, wavy, pale lilac ...trips and fill the space in between ...ith irregular, clear glass pieces.

## Rear vase

1 Cut the clear glass in half and then into irregular triangles using the glass nibbling pincers. Cut the leftovers and the milky, ribbed and light grey glass into 5mm (³⁄₁₆in) sqaures (see page 21).

2 Work downwards from the top of the vase, row by row. First stick on two rows of clear, square glass pieces, then stick on the wavy, light grey line. Some of the glass squares must be cut into conical shapes (see page 26) so that the wavy line is continuous. Finally, fill the areas in between with clear triangles.

3 Then lay the wavy line using clear, milky and light grey glass. Next stick on the zigzag row, then the lines that connect it to the one above. Fill the remainder of the surface with clear triangles. Stick on the lowest, light grey line and lay from the diagonal strip above it. This provides free areas for filling with clear triangles.

4 Leave everything to dry overnight and grout with old rose grouting compound. After 24 hours, clean and polish the mosaic.

**LEVEL OF DIFFICULTY**
◔◔◔

**MOTIF HEIGHT**
Approx. 23cm (9in)

**MATERIALS**

- Glass vase, diameter 24cm (9½in), neck diameter 8cm (3⅛in), 23cm (9in) high
- Transparent glass leftovers: pale lilac, 20 x 30cm (8 x 12in), smooth old rose, 10 x 30cm (4 x 12in), ribbed old rose, 10 x 30cm (4 x 12in), and clear, 20 x 30cm (8 x 12in) (front vase)
- Transparent glass leftovers: smooth clear, 10 x 30cm (4 x 12in), ribbed clear, 15 x 30cm (6 x 12in), milky clear, 10 x 30cm (4 x 12in), and pale grey, 15 x 30cm (6 x 12in)
- Silicone adhesive

**TEMPLATE**
Page 128

## Advice

◆ Silicone marks on the glass must be removed straight away using undiluted washing-up liquid. The adhesive cannot be removed from clothing, so be sure to wear an apron or an old shirt when working.

◆ Make sure you select glass leftovers that are of the same thickness.

# DECORATIVE SIDE-TABLE PIECES

## Tips & Tricks

◆ The Tiffany glass pieces are either mirrored or opaque. Although they are very effective, they don't let the light through. Use transparent glass and silicone adhesive for lantern glass. Wash off any marks left by the adhesive immediately using undiluted washing-up liquid.

◆ You can partially use tesserae, as shown on the lantern glass in the photo opposite.

### LEVEL OF DIFFICULTY
☉

### MOTIF SIZES

Glasses approx. 10cm (4in) high

Plate diameter approx. 33cm (13in)

### MATERIALS FOR DECORATIVE GLASSES

◆ 1 lantern glass each, 10cm (4in) high
◆ Approx. 70 Tiffany glass pieces in red, orange and yellow, 2cm (¾in) square, and 52 millefiori discs in red and ochre, diameter 7mm ($5/16$in)
◆ Tiffany glass pieces in 13 x brown, approx. 2 x 1cm (¾ x ⅜ in), and approx. 3 x ochre and yellow, approx. 2cm (¾in) square, plus 20 millefiori discs in brown, diameter 5mm ($3/16$in) (brown glass)
◆ Cement-based tile adhesive in white
◆ Colour pigment in ochre or green

### DECORATIVE PLATE

◆ Flat metal plate with wide rim in bronze, diameter 33cm (13in)
◆ Tiffany glass in approx. 10 x red, 20 x orange, 15 x yellow and 70 x cream, approx. 2cm (¾in) square
◆ Tiffany glass pieces in red, approx. 2.5 x 2cm (1 x ¾in)
◆ Millefiori discs in 16 x brown and 12 x red, diameter 5–6mm ($3/16$–¼in)
◆ Cement-based tile adhesive in white
◆ Colour pigment in ochre

### TEMPLATE
Page 128

## Decorative glasses

1 Cut the Tiffany glass into 1–1.5cm (⅜–⅝ in) squares and 2cm (¾in) strips using a glass cutter and metal ruler or support board o the glass nibbling pincers (see page 24).

2 Mix the adhesive powder with colour pigments and water to for a soft compound. Apply this step by step to the glass, starting at th lower edge.

3 Work using the direct method (see page 28 onwards), but with a raised adhesive bed 4–5mm ($5/32$–$3/16$in) thick, pressing in the tesserae with tweezers. Alternate Tiffany glass pieces and millefior discs and pieces, as in the photo. The glasses are left ungrout

## Decorative plate

1 Mix a very small amount of adhesive powder with a pinch of colour pigment and stir in some water to form a smooth compound. Then apply about a 3–4mm (⅛in) thick layer to the plate (see page 32–33).

2 Cut the stones as in the photo using the glass nibbling pincers o a glass cutter.

3 Place the large, square red stone in the middle of the plate and lay the petals from here outwards. If necessary, the pattern can be transferred onto the damp mortar (see page 13). Again, use the direct method with a raised adhesive bed (see Step 3 above). For each petal, alternate five square red stones with as many angular orange stones and press into the adhesive compound. Use tweezers

4 Inside the leaf place two pointed glass stones and six or eight millefiori discs.

5 Lay the border and finally the red petals with cream pieces in th *Opus Vermiculatum* around them (see page 14). Then fill the area between the petals.

# FLOOR-STANDING MIRROR

## Tips & Tricks

◆ You can also use the tendril motif to create a stool or table top, for example, like the one in the photo below. The template for this is on page 130.

◆ The mirror frame was professionally made from aluminium; a picture framing shop will do this for you.

**LEVEL OF DIFFICULTY**
☺☺☺

**MOTIF HEIGHT**
Approx. 1.6m (1¾yd)

**MATERIALS**

◆ MDF board at least 1.6cm (⅝in) thick, 1.6m x 70cm (1¾yd x 2ft 3½in)
◆ Mirror, 1cm (⅜in) thick, 1.5m x 60cm (4ft 11in x 23¾in)
◆ Approx. 2,000 each of marble stones in light blue and shades of white, 1cm (⅜in)
◆ Smalti or glass tesserae in 25 each x red, orange, yellow, shades of green and blue
◆ Approx. 20 silver tesserae (with light blue background or mirror shards), 1cm (⅜in) square
◆ Approx. 20 gold tesserae, 1cm (⅜in) square
◆ Approx. 10 glass nuggets in shades of green, blue and red, diameters 1.5cm (⅝in) and 2cm (¾in)
◆ Cement-based tile adhesive in grey
◆ Silicone adhesive
◆ Masking tape
◆ Jigsaw and blade
◆ Adhesive primer

**TEMPLATE**
Page 128

1 Saw the frame from the MDF board; the frame is approx. 10cm (4in) wide. Coat with adhesive primer and leave to dry.

2 Attach the mirror to the reverse using silicone adhesive. Leave to dry thoroughly.

3 Cover the mirror with newspaper and stick to the sides using masking tape. Also protect the edges of the frame with masking tape so that they are not soiled while you are working.

4 Cut the tesserae; you will also need to cut longer strips from the coloured glass (see page 20 onwards).

5 The mirror frame is covered using the direct technique, placing the tesserae close together, and is left ungrouted. Transfer the pattern onto the wood and start laying the tesserae. Only apply as much adhesive as you can cover in 10 minutes. The thickness of the adhesive depends upon the material: when using ready-made tesserae from marble and glass, it is about 3–4mm (⅛in) thick; for pieces you have split yourself using the hammer and awl, about 1cm (⅜in) thick. Only mix up as much tile adhesive as you can use in 10 minutes. Do not mix the full amount for the whole mirror frame in one go, otherwise the adhesive will dry out.

6 Start by laying the tendrils. Begin with a leaf and make the tendril by toning down from light to dark and back. Insert gold and silver stones at intervals. Then place little twigs along the branch and decorate them with little beads and millefiori discs.

7 Next lay the inner and outer borders, placing glass nuggets in the corners of the inner border. Finally, lay the surface between the tendrils and the edge in the *Opus Vermiculatum* (see page 14).

8 Work in this way, tendril by tendril. Gold and silver pieces are laid between the upper and lower corner motifs.

# TABLE WITH ROSES

## Tips & Tricks

◆ If you want to use the table outdoors, you should use a piece of concrete as the backing.

◆ Turning the base requires two people.

◆ Little pictures can also be created using a rose motif (see small photo below) you can use them as coasters. You could, alternatively, have a tiler lay several of these pictures in a tiled wall.

**LEVEL OF DIFFICULTY**
◎◎◎

**MOTIF SIZE**
Diameter approx. 60cm (23¾in)

**MATERIALS**

◆ MDF board, 2.5cm (1in) thick, 60cm (23¾in) square

◆ Approx. 12 glass tesserae each in shades of red and orange, 2cm (¾in) square

◆ Approx. 12 glass tesserae in shades of pink and lilac, 2cm (¾in) square

◆ Approx. 30 glass tesserae in shades of green, 2cm (¾in) square

◆ Approx. 10 glass tesserae in shades of blue, 2cm (¾in)

◆ Approx. 100 stoneware tesserae in black, 2.3cm (15⁄16in) square

◆ Approx. 330 stoneware tesserae in white, 2.3cm (15⁄16in) square

◆ Mosaic glue or flour paste (see page 39)

◆ Cement-based flexible tile adhesive

◆ Grouting compound in grey

◆ Adhesive primer

◆ Jigsaw with fine blade

◆ Large piece of plastic

**TEMPLATE**
Page 128

1  Saw a circle 59.3cm (23¼in) in diameter from the MDF board using the jigsaw. Then paint the board with adhesive primer, not forgetting the edge.

2  Retain 140 tesserae for the white edge and cut about 100 stones in half for the wave-like pattern. Cut the rest as polygons, that is, into irregular shapes (see page 60). Stick the pieces for the table to onto the paper design with mosaic glue using the indirect method (see page 38 onwards). Start by laying the roses and finally the polygons for the background, then lay the line around the outer edge using whole mosaic stones. Leave to dry and cut off the excess paper with a cutter.

3  For the wave-like pattern, first lay the square white and black pieces for the spiral lines (cut into quarters, see page 80) and then, from the halved pieces, cut and lay the matching conical pieces (see page 26).

4  Stick the edging stones with tile adhesive to the edge of the MDF board (see page 34) and leave to dry for at least 24 hours. To stick the edging stones, lay the set mosaic exactly onto the MDF board (mark the position so that the edging pieces will meet one another later) and stick the stones butting up to each other. Lay plastic sheeting between the mosaic and the MDF board as protection.

5  Mix the grouting compound so that it is free of lumps and not too runny (see page 33, Step 6). Mix the adhesive so that it is soft and free of lumps (see page 32, Step 3). Apply an even layer of adhesive about 1–2mm (1⁄16in) thick over the MDF board.

6  Place the mosaic laid on paper onto a mobile base (such as a piece of wood) and grout from the reverse. Lay the MDF board covered with adhesive onto the reverse grouted mosaic. Press together, turn over and firm by knocking with a trowel (see page 41) Also knock the edging with the trowel so that the horizontally placed edging stones butt up to the vertical ones (around the edge of the table top). They should not jut out.

7  Once the grouting compound and adhesive have set, carefully remove the paper. Finish according to the step-by-step instructions on page 41.

# CANDLESTICKS

## Candlestick

**1** Cut the individual motifs to shape using the mosaic nippers (do not break up with the hammer, as too much of the pattern will be destroyed), making circles, squares or longer pieces, no longer than 2cm (¾in), according to the pattern.

**2** When you have enough motifs, stick on in rows, working from the bottom up. Cover each piece with sufficient adhesive and lay. Mix the adhesive a little thicker so that the curves of the candlestick and the uneven thickness of the china is easier to even out. With larger mosaic pieces, apply a pea-sized amount of adhesive underneath in the middle; when you press it on the adhesive, it will spread across the base.

**3** The last row at the top must be stuck at least 5mm (³⁄₁₆in) over the edge so that the pieces that are later laid horizontally will join up neatly.

**4** Leave to dry for at least 36 hours, as the adhesive is very thick in places. Then grout with white grout. Polish with a soft cloth 24 hours later.

## Rose dish

**1** Cut out the individual motifs using mosaic nippers (see pages 22 and 27). When you have enough motifs, try out a design to find the best layout that looks good. Then prepare the edge pieces, 1cm (³⁄₈in) square to 1 x 2cm (³⁄₈ x ¾in).

**2** Cover the dish using the direct method (see page 51). First glue the edge pieces to the outer edge of the dish. Then lay the flower motifs, working from the middle outwards.

**3** Cut the gold tesserae into irregular pieces using the glass nibbling pincers (see page 26) and stick them into the larger gaps, evenly distributed.

**4** Leave everything to dry overnight and then grout. Polish with a soft cloth 24 hours later.

**LEVEL OF DIFFICULTY**

**MOTIF HEIGHT/SIZE**
Candlestick approx. 36cm (14¼in) high
Rose dish diameter approx. 31cm (12¼in)

**MATERIALS FOR CANDLESTICK**
- Ceramic candlestick, 36cm (14¼in) high
- Approx. 15 plates with small motifs
- Cement-based file adhesive in white
- Grouting compound in white

**ROSE DISH**
- Rose dish, diameter 31cm (12¼in)
- Approx. 12 china plates with a strong central motif
- 2 glass tesserae in gold, 1cm (³⁄₈in) square
- Cement-based adhesive in white
- Grouting compound in white

## Tips & Tricks

◆ Instead of china plates, you could use small, patterned tiles.

◆ Even a decorative sphere can be covered with china fragments, as in the photo below right. For larger objects, work on one half first, leave to dry, then cover the second half. Place in a dish to make it easier to cover with mosaic.

# ROUND MIRROR

## Advice

◆ Make sure that the ceramic tesserae are of an equal thickness. Use thin pieces of mirror.

◆ To hang the mirror, fix a metal attachment to the rear using silicone adhesive (see small photo below).

◆ You can also use transparent coloured glass for the mirror – it will sparkle attractively due to the mirrored glass underneath.

### LEVEL OF DIFFICULTY
◔◔

### MOTIF SIZE
Diameter approx. 55cm (21¾in)

### MATERIALS
◆ Round mirror, diameter 55cm (21¾in)
◆ Ceramic pieces: 25 x sparkling ultramarine, 2 each x matt ultramarine and sparkling deep blue, 3 each x sparkling pale turquoise and bluey-grey, plus sky blue and matt light blue, 4 x sparkling turquoise, 5 x sparkling light green, 8 each x sparkling bluey-grey and turquoise green, plus matt bluey-grey, 10 x sparkling mid-blue and 40 x matt deep blue, 2.5cm (1in) square
◆ 1 glass nugget each in light blue, dark blue and iridescent blue, diameter 1.5cm (⅝in)
◆ 25 round glass buttons in green, diameter 1.3cm (½in)
◆ 20 metal buttons in light grey, 1.3cm (½in) square
◆ 13 hexagonal decorative beads, 1.5 x 2.5cm (⅝ x 1in)
◆ Mirror leftovers, 10 x 30cm (4 x 12in)
◆ Silicone adhesive
◆ Grout in anthracite

### TEMPLATE
Page 128

1 Draw the template onto the mirror using a permanent felt pen. Cut out the individual pieces and use as templates. Cover the mirror with silicone adhesive using the direct method (see page 28 onwards; step-by-step instructions on pages 32–33).

2 Cut the tesserae diagonally into quarters or eighths using the pincers (see page 84) or cut into 16 squares (see page 80, bottom left photo – cut through each stone again).

3 Score the piece of mirrored glass in strips 1cm (⅜in) wide using the glass cutter and split with the breaking pincers (see page 24). Nip triangles out of these strips using glass nibbling pincers (see page 21).

4 Apply an even 1mm (¹/₃₂in) layer of silicone adhesive using the spatula and continue piece by piece. Only apply to an area that can be covered in 10–15 minutes.

5 Start by laying the circles: stick the glass nuggets in the middle, then lay the frame with buttons or decorative pieces and fill the surface with mirror pieces.

6 Work on the curves between the circles. Lay the edges again first and then fill the surface in between. Edge the exterior wavy lines with four or five rows of blue squares; fill the remaining inner areas with stepped blue triangles. Finally, create the dark blue border with sparkling and matt triangles. Create a clean, closely placed line when sticking the tesserae so that there is no need for a grouted edge.

7 Leave to dry overnight and then grout.

# WATER FEATURE

## Tips & Tricks

◆ This indoor water feature is great for using up leftover pieces; simply use all the pieces you still have. However, make sure that they are of the same size.

◆ Water pumps for indoor water features are easily obtainable from DIY stores or from garden centres.

### LEVEL OF DIFFICULTY
◶◶

### MOTIF SIZE
Dish diameter approx. 38cm (15in)

### MATERIALS

◆ Ceramic indoor water feature: dish diameter 38cm (15in), 9cm (3½in) high, and matching sphere, diameter 23cm (9in), 15cm (6in) high

◆ Approx. 1,560 glass tesserae in dark blue, 1cm (⅜in) square

◆ Approx. 620 ceramic tesserae in eggshell colours, 1cm (⅜in) square

◆ 152 coloured glass tesserae in various colours, 1.5cm (⅝in) square

◆ Coloured leftover fragments, in total approx. 20 x 60cm (8 x 23¾in)

◆ Cement-based tile adhesive in mid-grey

◆ Grouting compound in dark blue

◆ Water pump for indoor water features

1 The dish is covered inside and out using the direct method – the sphere is just covered on the outside (see page 51). Apply a 2mm (³⁄₃₂in) thick layer of adhesive and smooth using a spatula, only covering an area that you can lay within 10–20 minutes.

2 When covering the dish, start at the top edge with five rows of dark blue stones; make the transition to the base of the dish with two eggshell-coloured rows and then 10 rings of circles in dark blue. One circle remains in the middle about 10cm in diameter (4in) and i filled with coloured glass fragments.

3 Then cover the outside of the dish from the bottom edge. Start with five rows of eggshell-coloured stones and then lay two rows of coloured stones.

4 The sphere is covered from the bottom upwards. First lay six rows of dark blue stones and a row of eggshell-coloured ones. Then stick on long glass fragments about 1.5–2cm (⅝–¾in long) and finally fill the surface up to the water hole with small triangles and irregular shapes with edge lengths of approximately 5mm (³⁄₁₆in).

5 Leave to dry for 24 hours and then grout. Clean the next day and insert the water pump.

# FOUND OBJECTS

## Mirror frame

1. Paint the wooden frame with adhesive primer and leave to dry.

2. Cover a small area with adhesive about 2mm (³/₃₂in) thick. Only cover an area that you can lay within 10 minutes.

3. Press the mosaic pieces into the adhesive bed. Work using the direct method (see page 28 onwards). Start at the edge of the mirror and lay the finished edges of ceramic pieces or other straight-edged pieces as an edging. Then fill in, working from the outside in. Saw the pieces of wood to the right size.

4. Wipe off any excess adhesive and sprinkle quartz sand into the open gaps. Shake off the excess quartz sand.

5. Finally, paint a thin layer of adhesive onto the outside edge of the mirror frame and press into quartz sand.

## Box

1. The box is covered with found objects using the direct method (see page 28 onwards), like the frame.

2. Paint a small area with softly mixed adhesive (only as much as you can cover in 10 minutes). Stick the first pieces preferably around the opening on the top, selecting straight edges on the mosaic pieces for the edging. Wipe off any excess adhesive and sprinkle quartz sand into the open gaps. Shake off the excess quartz sand.

3. Then fill the rest of the surface. Curved tesserae are very useful for the edges, for example, from crockery or small pieces. Fill again any free areas between the mosaic pieces with quartz sand.

4. Continue laying the lower edge. Make sure that you achieve a very straight edge and then finally fill in the remaining areas.

### LEVEL OF DIFFICULTY
◔

### MOTIF HEIGHTS
Mirror frame approx. 26cm (10¼in)

Box approx. 10cm (4in)

### MATERIALS
- Mirror frame with wide edge, 26cm (10¼in) square, and wooden box, 30 x 15 x 8cm (12 x 6 x 3⅛in)
- Found objects and leftover pieces: tile fragments, pieces of bottle glass from the beach, shells, pebbles, bits of wood and so on
- Cement-based tile adhesive or dispersion adhesive in white
- Quartz sand
- Small wood saw, if needed

## Tips & Tricks

◆ Fragile shells should be filled with a mixture of two parts tile adhesive and one part quartz sand, blended with water (see page 11), before they are stuck on. This also gives the shells a larger adhesive surface.

◆ You can obtain a wide range of suitable picture frames and boxes from specialist craft shops. Always choose your pieces of wood with care. Do not use woodchip or papier mâché, as they are not stable enough.

# BREAKFAST TRAY

## Tips & Tricks

◆ If your tray is larger than the pattern, you can simply create a wider outer border.

◆ Beginners can start with extracts from the patchwork pattern, for example, with coasters using hearts, flowers or spiral motifs.

### LEVEL OF DIFFICULTY
⊙⊙⊙

### MOTIF SIZE
Approx. 44cm (17¼in) wide

### MATERIALS

◆ Ceramic tesserae: 4 x yellowy-orange, 7 x white and 5 x brown, 8 each x pink, fuchsia, yellow and midnight blue, 9 each x black and green, 20 x red, 40 x lilac and 70 x mid-blue, 2.5cm (1in) square

◆ Breakfast tray approx 25 x 44cm (10 x 17¼in) (area to be covered)

◆ Silicone adhesive

◆ Grouting compound in beige

### TEMPLATE
Page 129

**1** The tray can be laid in both the direct method (for materials of the same thickness) and the indirect method, the latter providing a completely level surface (transfer a mirror image of the pattern onto the design, see page 39).

**2** Cut out the mosaic tesserae: cut the mid-blue and some of the red stones into quarters for the inner background (see the photo with the yellow stones below left, stage 3), and cut the black and white stones into ninths, as well as those red and green stones for the edging of the little patterns. Cut the lilac-coloured stones for the outer edge as in the photo below left (yellow stones). For the petals cut strips of the right size and nip into shape (draw the shape onto the reverse).

**3** Work outwards from the centre. For the direct method, transfer the pattern onto the tray. Apply an even 2mm (³⁄₃₂in) layer of silicone adhesive, only covering an area that you can lay within 15 minutes (see page 28 onwards). If you are working in the indirect method, lay the mirror image of the mosaic on paper and then stick onto the tray (see page 38 onwards, or if you are working using the reciprocal technique, see page 42).

**4** First lay the butterfly (see page 14), then the blue area. Finally, add the black and white edging and lay the frame for the small patterned area. Fill in the remaining areas; for the patterned areas, lay the motif first and then the background.

**5** If laying the mosaic in the indirect method, stick to the wooden tray. Whichever method, leave overnight to dry and then grout. The beige grouting compound works well with the light wooden frame. Clean and polish 24 hours later.

# COLOURFUL FISH

## Tips & Tricks

◆ A large fish can also be used as a mirror frame. Saw a hole and fix the mirror behind it using silicone adhesive or mirror clips (see small photo below).

◆ The fish are made using a raised adhesive bed (see Step 2) and are left ungrouted. You can also lay and grout them in the usual way following the step-by-step instructions on pages 32–33, using glass tesserae only.

### LEVEL OF DIFFICULTY
◔◔

### MOTIF HEIGHT
Approx. 15–25cm (6–10in)

### MATERIALS

◆ MDF board, 1cm (⅜ in) thick, 20.5 x 12cm (8 x 4¾in) (red and yellow fish)⚇ 28 x 19cm (11 x 7½in) (green fish) and 15 x 24cm (6 x 9½in) (seagrass)

◆ Approx. 220–375 smalti or glass tesserae in shades of green, red, orange and blue (depending on the size of the fish), 1cm (⅜in) square

◆ Cement-based tile adhesive in white

◆ Colour pigment in blue, light green and dark green

◆ Grouting compound in white, if needed

◆ Jigsaw with fine blade

◆ Sandpaper

◆ Several metal picture hooks, approx. 3cm (1⅛in) wide

### TEMPLATE
Page 129

1 Saw the fish out of wood and smooth the edges with sandpaper. Fix one or two picture hooks to the reverse. Paint adhesive primer onto the wooden surface and allow to dry.

2 All the fish are made in the same way but in different colour combinations. Lay the tesserae in the direct method (see page 28 onwards), but use a raised adhesive base, that is, apply the adhesive more thickly about 4–5mm (³⁄₁₆in) and just press the mosaic pieces into it. Place the pieces close to one another.

3 Cut the mosaic pieces according to the material used using the smalti pincers or a glass cutter or the glass nibbling pincers (see pages 24 and 26). You will need some round pieces for the eyes (see page 27), long pieces for the mouth, quite a lot of conically cut pieces for making the circular shapes (see page 26) and lots of square tesserae (see photos on page 80).

4 First make the eyes (working from the round centre outwards), then the mouth and finally the pattern (see also page 14). Next create the border and then fill the remaining surface. Only apply to the surface as much adhesive as you can cover in 10 minutes. Then leave to dry overnight.

5 To make the wooden edge, mix colour pigment into the adhesive and add water to form a soft compound. Paint on using a brush or spatula. Leave to dry thoroughly.

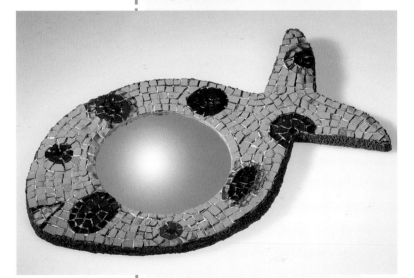

# BLUE TABLE

## Tips & Tricks

◆ Circles are easiest to draw using a pair of compasses. For larger circles, however, their radius is not big enough, which is where home-made compasses come into their own. Knock a nail into the centre of a plank of wood and tie a piece of string to it. Attach a pencil to the other end of the string – simply adjust the distance between the nail and the pencil depending on the desired radius. Draw the circle by moving the pencil around the nail. Make sure that the string does not tie itself around the nail, or you will end up with a spiral shape.

### LEVEL OF DIFFICULTY
◎◎◎

### MOTIF HEIGHT
Diameter approx. 62cm (24½in)

### MATERIALS
◆ Slab of concrete 4.5cm (1¾in) thick, diameter 61cm (24in)
◆ Ceramic tesserae: approx. 140 x dark blue and approx. 66 each x turquoise and pale turquoise, 2.5cm (1in) square
◆ Glass tesserae: 150 x gold and 80 x copper, 1cm (⅜in) square
◆ Approx. 235 glass mosaic stones in dark turquoise, 2cm (¾in) square
◆ Approx. 66 glass mosaic stones in water green, 2.5cm (1in) square
◆ Approx. 100 hexagonal tesserae in turquoise, 2.5 x 3cm (1 x 1⅛in)
◆ Two-component adhesive or frost-proof, cement-based tile adhesive
◆ Grouting compound in black
◆ Mosaic glue or flour paste (see page 39)

### TEMPLATE
Page 127

1 The table is made using the indirect method (see the step-by-step instructions on pages 39–41). Place the paper with the design on a wooden board and fix with adhesive tape. Draw a circle 61cm (24in) in diameter and in the centre draw a star. Glue on the tesserae, working from the outside in, using mosaic glue.

2 First stick the hexagonal turquoise tesserae with the points butted up against one another and place gold triangles in between (cut about 65 diagonal pieces in half, see the photo below right, stage 2; for larger stones, cut in half again as necessary).

3 Then set a ring of water green tesserae and finally a ring of dark turquoise. Leave a strip about 5cm (2in) wide free (draw out if necessary), then lay another dark turquoise ring and one from hexagonal stones and copper triangles (using about 35 stones). Fill the areas in between with small squares (about 130 tesserae in turquoise and pale turquoise cut into ninths, see page 80).

4 Next lay the two stars from irregular copper and gold triangular shapes, first the contours and then fill in the other areas. Fill the area around the stars up to the turquoise ring with irregular dark blue triangles (cut from about 60 stones).

5 Apply the glue with a toothed spatula about 2mm (³⁄₃₂in) thick to the slab of concrete and stick on the reverse mosaic. Then pull off the paper and allow the work to dry.

6 The border is formed after laying the mosaic (see page 34). Paint with adhesive piece by piece and cover with dark turquoise and dark blue tesserae. Remove the excess adhesive and leave to dry for 24 hours. Grout, then clean and polish the next day.

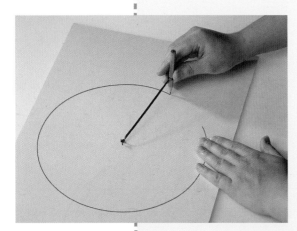

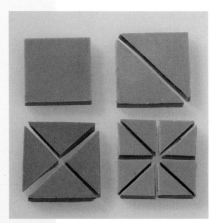

# MIRROR FRAME

**1** Saw a piece out of the MDF board that is a little smaller than the mirror ensuring you allow a border approximately 10cm (4in wide). Attach two picture hooks to the reverse, capable of holding a weight of about 10kg (22lb).

**2** You can have the wooden board made into a frame by a specialist (for example, at a picture framing shop). Alternatively, you could make it yourself with cut and stained planks of wood (see page 34). To prevent the wooden planks from being soiled, cover with masking tape. Paint the surfaces to be decorated with mosaic with adhesive primer (see page 29).

**3** Trace the drawing of the tendril motif onto tracing paper using a water-soluble felt pen (see Expert Tip, page 13). Work using the direct method (see page 28 onwards), but use a raised adhesive bed, that is, apply the adhesive in a layer about 4–5mm (3/16in) thick. When pressing in the stones, it will rise into the gaps so that the work does not need to be grouted. Cut the marble stones for the motif with 5mm (3/16in) long sides; also cut out the cream stones (up to the inner and outer edging stones).

**4** Mix the mortar compound. Use cement powder and sand in equal parts in a dry state and mix thoroughly. Then add the lime and water and carefully stir with a trowel. The resulting mixture should form a fine, soft compound.

**5** Apply a layer of the mixed mortar to a corner of the picture frame using a spatula. Spray the backing with a little water beforehand. Press part of the drawing onto it. Lay the tendril and the first flower. Then fill the background with cream marble stones.

**6** Apply some more mortar and continue laying the motif. Leave to dry overnight, then stick the mirror to the reverse using silicone adhesive (if it is already fitted into the frame, cover with newspaper while working on it and fix with masking tape).

## LEVEL OF DIFFICULTY
◐◐

## MOTIF HEIGHT
Approx. 60cm (23¾in)

## MATERIALS
- MDF board, 1.6cm (⅝in), 42.5 x 57.5cm (16¾ x 22¾in)
- Mirror, 20 x 35cm (8 x 13¾in)
- Approx. 1,800 marble stones in cream, 1cm (⅜in) square
- Marble tesserae in 650 x dark brown and 350 x rose, 1cm (⅜in) square
- Wood stain in dark brown
- 2 picture hooks, approx. 3cm (1⅛in) wide
- Masking tape
- Lime, white cement and sand (for adhesive mortar) or cement-based tile adhesive in beige
- Silicone adhesive
- Adhesive primer
- Water spray

## TEMPLATE
Page 128

## Tips & Tricks

◆ You can also use the tendril motif to decorate a table top.

# FLORAL DISHES

## Advice

◆ You can obtain metal dishes from furniture stores or homeware sections in department stores. Alternatively, you can use a china dish. Do not forget the adhesive primer (see page 29).

**LEVEL OF DIFFICULTY**
◔◔◔

**MOTIF SIZE**

Diameter approx. 31.5cm (12½in)

**MATERIALS FOR DAISY DISH**

◆ Metal dish, diameter 31.5cm (12½in)

◆ Ceramic tesserae: 5 each x yellow and beige, 24 x eggshell-coloured, 25 each x light green, pink and lilac, and 50 x white, 2.5cm (1in) square

◆ Transparent silicone adhesive

◆ Grouting compound in old rose (from mixing beige, red and yellow)

**MEADOW FLOWERS**

◆ Metal dish, diameter 31.5cm (12½in)

◆ Ceramic tesserae: 2 each x black and white, 4 each x whitish-yellow, pale yellow and ochre, 9 x yellow, 10 x deep orange, 14 x fuchsia, 15 x pink, 18 x red, 20 x mid-green, 26 x light green and 32 x orange, 2.5cm (1in) square

◆ Transparent silicone adhesive

◆ Grouting compound in red, old rose (from mixing beige, red and yellow) and green

**TEMPLATE**
Page 130

## Daisy dish

1 Transfer the pattern onto the metal dish (use adhesive primer if necessary). Cover using the direct method (see the step-by-step instructions on page 32).

2 For the centre of the flowers, quarter the yellow tesserae and shape into round pieces using the mosaic nippers (see page 27). Cut the white, eggshell and beige-coloured tesserae into small triangles (see pages 80 and 84).

3 Apply the silicone adhesive to each area and spread evenly 1mm ($\frac{1}{32}$in) thick using a small spatula. Start at the centre by sticking on the beige flowers, then fill in the background and lay the next row of flowers (the second row is eggshell-coloured and the last row is white). Continue in this way until the plate is covered. After sticking on the last row of flowers, lay the border at an even 3mm ($\frac{1}{8}$in) depth from the edge of the dish, then fill in the background.

4 Leave to dry overnight and then grout with old rose. Clean the mosaic with diluted vinegar, rinse and polish 24 hours later.

## Meadow flowers

1 Prepare the dish as described in Step 1 above. Then cut the tesserae. Cut the orange stones into long, irregular strips, and the light green and mid-green into small triangles (see page 84). Cut the ochre stones in half and then cut into small, pointed triangles (about 10 pieces per stone). Cut the rose stones into conical shapes (see page 26). Cut white, pale yellow, yellow and black tesserae into circles in various sizes, the majority with a diameter of 3–5mm ($\frac{1}{8}$–$\frac{3}{16}$in) some for the large flower on the right are a little larger. Divide out the red tesserae in the centre and make poppy petals (draw the shape on the reverse), and divide the orange stones into thirds and cut out. Cut the fuchsia stones into circles and halve (see page 27) or cut in half diagonally and then nip into shape.

2 Start with the large flower when gluing: lay the centre of the flower about 3mm ($\frac{1}{8}$in) from the edge of the dish and work from there out, sticking the petals pointing outwards, also including the green pieces for the background. Make sure that the border is straight and always 3mm ($\frac{1}{8}$in) away from the edge of the dish.

3 Leave overnight to dry. Then grout: first the centre of the poppy in red, then the large orange flower in old rose. Leave to dry overnight, then grout the rest using the green grouting compound. Leave to dry again overnight and clean (see also page 19).

# IDEAS FOR OUTDOORS

# GARDEN SPHERE

## arden sphere

Prime the sphere – there is no need to prime if you are using a ncrete sphere – and leave to dry.

The sphere is covered using the direct method (see page 51). ply a layer of adhesive about 1–2mm ( 1/16 in) thick. Only apply as uch adhesive as you can cover within 10 minutes.

Cut a small supply of stones; for the top part of the sphere, you ll need mainly conical-cut pieces (see page 26); around the iddle of the sphere, you can also use rectangular and square- aped pieces.

Cover the sphere, working from the top in the middle, beginning ith a pebble. Position the stones at even intervals, working your ay downwards in a spiral, using coloured stones; around the ntre of the sphere, alternate shades of grey and brown. Also insert irrored glass pieces.

Only cover half of the sphere and leave to dry for 24 hours. Then rn over and place on thick foam while you cover the other half in e same way.

Leave the fully laid sphere for 24 hours to dry and then grout. rout and clean one half first, then the other half. You do not need leave any drying time in between. Use a small brush to help ith the cleaning after grouting. Dip it briefly in water and use to oisten stones that are deeply set and covered with grout. Mop up ny liquid immediately with a sponge cloth or a sponge.

## rog

Paint adhesive primer onto the ceramic figure and leave to dry. ut the glass tesserae into irregular pieces about 1cm (3/8 in) in size sing glass nibbling pincers or a glass cutter (see pages 24 and 26).

Cover the figure using the direct method as described on page 51. tart with the coloured edges (mouth) and then work on the body, yes and legs.

Once the adhesive has dried, grout with grey grouting compound nd clean thoroughly. If the frog is to stand outdoors, make sure that ou use frostproof materials.

### LEVEL OF DIFFICULTY
◌◌◌

### MOTIF SIZES
Sphere approx. 25cm (10in) diameter
Frog approx. 14cm (5½in) high

### MATERIALS FOR THE SPHERE
- Concrete sphere or frostproof ceramic sphere, 25cm (10in) diameter
- Approx. 1,600 marble cubes in grey, brown and beige, 1cm (3/8 in) square
- Approx. 200 smalti in shades of brown and red
- Pebble
- Frostproof tile adhesive in grey
- Frostproof grouting compound in grey
- Adhesive primer, if needed

### FROG
- Ceramic or Styropor® figure, 14cm (5½in) high
- Cement-based tile adhesive in grey
- 2 glass nuggets in blue, 1.5cm (5/8 in) diameter
- Approx. 240 glass tesserae in shades of green, 2cm (¾in) square
- Adhesive primer
- Grouting compound in grey

## Tips & Tricks

- To work on the sphere, place it on a plinth so that it is at eye level.

- Although fairly expensive, a natural sponge is useful to use when cleaning.

- To work out the surface area of a sphere, apply this formula: surface = 4 π (3.14) r² (radius squared).

# DECORATIVE STONES

## Tips & Tricks

◆ These little stones are good for decorating the windowsill or the living room. You could also cover fairly large stones to put in the garden, but make sure that you use frostproof materials only.

**LEVEL OF DIFFICULTY**
☉

**MOTIF SIZE**
Approx. 7–10cm (2¾–4in) diameter

**MATERIALS**

◆ Pebbles in various sizes, 7–10cm (2¾–4in) diameter

◆ Glass nuggets in orange, 2cm (¾in) diameter, and glass or ceramic tesserae leftovers in light green, shades of yellow and orange (yellow stone)

◆ Glass nuggets in iridescent red, 1.5cm (⅝in) diameter, and glass or ceramic tesserae leftovers in ochre and red (ochre-coloured stone)

◆ Glass nuggets in white, 2cm (¾in) diameter, and glass or ceramic tesserae leftovers in yellow and red (red stone)

◆ Glass nuggets in white, 2cm (¾in) diameter, and glass or ceramic tesserae leftovers in yellow and red (red stone)

◆ Glass nuggets in yellow, 1.5cm (⅝in) diameter, and glass or ceramic tesserae leftovers in white, grey and shades of lilac (lilac-coloured stone)

◆ Cement-based tile adhesive in grey or white

◆ Grouting compound in mid-grey, yellow or red

**1** The mosaic objects are covered using the direct method (see page 51). Cover one side first and then, after leaving to dry, cover the other side.

**2a** Lay the nugget on the yellow stone and stick several narrow strips around it in a star shape 3mm x 1cm (⅛ x ⅜in). Next stick on small triangles and then a ring of square-cut yellow pieces with an edge length of about 5mm (³⁄₁₆in); also stick some narrow strips onto the sides. Leaving some distance, lay the ring around the widest part of the stone. Cover the reverse with irregular-cut glass pieces.

**2b** For the ochre-coloured stone, lay red triangular pieces in a flower around the glass nugget and fill the remaining area with ochre-coloured triangles. Lay two rings of squares around the widest part of the stone (after the first ring, leave to dry, then turn the stone over and continue working) and fill the reverse with irregular ochre-coloured pieces.

**2c** For the green stone, cut out circles about 1cm (⅜in) in diameter (see page 27) and stick strips about 1–1.5cm (⅜–⅝in) long around these and also triangles with an edge length of about 1cm (⅜in) to make small flowers. Fill the remaining area with small, green triangles.

**2d** The lilac-coloured and the red stones are each laid with a flower: stick on the nugget as the centre of the flower and lay strips rounded at the tip around it about 7cm (2¾in) wide, 1–1.5cm (⅜–⅝in) long and draw the shape on the back. Fill the remaining area with irregular-cut triangular pieces with an edge length of about 1cm (⅜in).

**3** Finally, grout the stones in the desired shade (see page 51).

# LANTERNS

Stick on the pattern following the photo, or sketch out on a
ece of paper and place inside the glass (when drawing out, refer
 the photo). Clean the glasses thoroughly before covering; there
ould be no grease on the surface.

Apply the silicone adhesive to an area at a time and spread over
enly with the spatula 1mm (1/32in) thick. The glass pieces need to
e pressed in well so that there are no air bubbles between the two
yers of glass. Leave 3mm (1/8in) of clear glass at the top and at the
ottom in order that the edge of the glass can be bevelled (the edge
ill be too sharp otherwise).

a For the round, pink glass (in the centre of the photo), first lay
e large glass nuggets and stick thin glass strips 3 x 6mm (1/8 x
in) around some of them to form three flowers. Fill the remaining
rea with the little glass spheres. For the round, orange-coloured
ntern, cut 12 5mm (3/16in) diameter circles from red glass 1 and
ick dark red, pointed triangles around these. Fill the remaining
rea with small, irregular, orange-coloured pieces nipped from 1cm
/8in) wide strips.

b For the triangular glasses, first lay the pattern – the wavy line
om little glass spheres and the vertical strips with nuggets at the
nd – and then fill the remaining area with small, triangular pieces.

c The small, oval glasses are made with a striped or checked
esign. For the glass in the front, first stick on the strips about 1cm
/8 in) wide and then fill all of the remaining areas with irregular,
ngular shapes. The other glass is simply covered with small,
rregular, angular pieces.

Leave for at least two hours to dry and then grout. After 24 hours,
inse with diluted vinegar and dry off.

## LEVEL OF DIFFICULTY
◐◐

## MOTIF SIZE
Approx. 7–9cm (2¾–3½in)

## MATERIALS FOR ROUND GLASSES

- Glass vessel, 7cm (2¾in) diameter, 9cm (3½in) high
- Transparent glass pieces in red, dark red and orange, in total approx. 5 x 20cm (2 x 8in) (orange with flowers)
- Glass nuggets: 9 x red, 1.5cm (5/8in) diameter, and 500 x pale pink, 3–5mm (1/8–3/16 in) diameter, plus transparent glass pieces in dark red, 25 x 1.5cm (1 x 5/8in) (pink with glass nuggets)
- Silicone adhesive
- Grouting compound in orange or pink

## TRIANGULAR GLASSES

- Glass vessel, 9cm (3½in) high
- 6 glass nuggets in red, diameter 1.5cm (5/8in), transparent glass piece in orange, approx. 9cm x 6mm (3½ x ¼in), and glass leftovers in shades of red, approx. 10 x 30cm (4 x 12in) (front glass with large nuggets)
- Approx. 50 glass nuggets in pale pink, 3–5mm (1/8–3/16in) diameter, transparent glass pieces in red and dark red, each 10 x 15cm (4 x 6in) (glass with mini-nuggets)
- Silicone adhesive
- Grouting compound in pink

## OVAL GLASSES

- Glass vessel, 9cm (3½in) wide, 6.5cm (2½in) high
- Transparent glass pieces in shades of red and orange, 10 x 30cm (4 x 12in)
- Silicone adhesive
- Grouting compound in orange or pink

## Advice

◆ Make sure that the material you use is transparent (Tiffany glass). Normal tesserae are opaque.

# FLOWERPOTS

## Tips & Tricks

◆ If you want to take a break from gluing, remove the excess adhesive from the object using a modeller's spatula.

◆ With a raised adhesive bed, the surface will not be uniformly even. If you prefer, you can work with a thinner adhesive layer and grout the mosaic after laying in the usual way (see page 51).

**LEVEL OF DIFFICULTY**
✪

**MOTIF HEIGHTS**
Flowerpot with lemons, 20cm (8in)
Flowerpot with olives, 19cm (7½in)
Small flowerpot, 14cm (5½in)

**MATERIALS FOR FLOWERPOT WITH LEMONS**
- Flowerpot, 26cm (10¼in) diameter, 20cm (8in) high
- Glass tesserae: approx. 180 x shades of white, cream and beige, approx. 50 x shades of green and 6 x shades of brown, 2cm (¾in) square
- 4 glass nuggets in green, approx. 2cm (¾in) diameter
- Cement-based tile adhesive in white
- Adhesive primer

**FLOWERPOT WITH OLIVES**
- Flowerpot, 14cm (5½in) diameter, 19cm (7½in) high
- Glass tesserae: approx. 70 x shades of green and 50 x shades of yellow, 2cm (¾in) square
- 4 glass nuggets in green, approx. 2cm (¾in) diameter
- Cement-based tile adhesive in white
- Adhesive primer

**SMALL FLOWERPOT**
- Flowerpot, 14cm (5½in) diameter, 14cm (5½in) high
- Glass tesserae: approx. 70 x shades of green and 50 x shades of yellow, 2cm (¾in) square
- Cement-based tile adhesive in white
- Structure paste in white
- Acrylic paint in terracotta
- Adhesive primer

**TEMPLATE**
Page 130

## Flowerpot with lemons

1 Paint the base with adhesive primer and leave to dry. Then transfer the outline of the sprig of lemons onto the flowerpot using carbon paper.

2 Cut the tesserae into shape according to the template and photo using the glass cutter or the glass nibbling pincers (see pages 24 and 26). You will need mainly strips, as well as some conical (see page 26) and square-cut pieces.

3 The flowerpot is covered with mosaic using the direct method (see page 48 onwards), but with a raised adhesive bed, that is, the adhesive is applied more thickly about 3mm(⅛in) thick and the tesserae are just pressed into it and left ungrouted. Only apply as much adhesive as you can cover within 10 minutes. Remove any excess adhesive with a spatula.

4 Start with laying the edge. Next work on the branch for the left lemon and then lay the lemon from the outside inwards. Use a pair of tweezers for this work.

5 Work on the leaf between the lemons, then the second lemon and the other parts of the motif. Leave to dry overnight.

6 Paint the free area of the motif with structure paste using a brush. Leave to dry overnight. Once it has dried, structure paste becomes watertight.

## Flowerpot with olives and small flowerpot

1 Prepare the flowerpot as described above and cut up a supply of little stones (see Steps 1 and 2; you will need squares and strips for the small flowerpot).

2 The flowerpots are covered in the same way using the direct method (see above), including the background. When laying, first work on creating the edging and the main motif and then fill in the area around them. Leave everything at least overnight to dry. The small pot is additionally coated with structure paste around the top edge and painted.

# BIRD BATH

## Tips & Tricks

◆ Even small plant pots look really pretty when covered with pebbles. You could also use terracotta ornaments available from DIY stores or garden centres and vary the colour of the grout, such as the grey and terracotta colours used here (a mixture of beige, deep red and ochre; see the small photos below).

## Advice

◆You can buy the china fish from shops or suppliers specializing in oriental goods.

**LEVEL OF DIFFICULTY**
◔

**MOTIF HEIGHT**
Approx. 40cm (15¾in)

**MATERIALS**
◆ Terracotta flowerpot, 29cm (11½in) diameter, 35cm (13¾in) high
◆ Terracotta saucer, 38cm (15in) diameter, 7cm (2¾in) high
◆ Pebbles in various colours, 5mm–3cm (³⁄₁₆in–1⅛in) diameter
◆ 2 ceramic mosaic tiles in dove grey, 20cm (8in) square
◆ 5 china fish in blue, 6cm (2⅜in) and 8cm (3⅛in) long respectively
◆ Cement-based tile adhesive in white
◆ Grouting compound in beige
◆ Adhesive primer
◆ Linseed oil and soft cloths
◆ Water spray

1 A few days before starting work, soak the stones overnight in water to clean them and rinse them well the next day. Then leave f[or] several days to dry out thoroughly. Finally, paint them with linseed oil and leave them again overnight to dry. Wipe off any excess oil the next day with a cloth. The colour of the stone will be all the more intense.

2 Paint the dish with adhesive primer (see page 29), and once it is dry, start sticking the tesserae using the direct method (see page 51). Only apply as much adhesive as you can cover in 10 minutes, applying it about 5mm (³⁄₁₆in) thick and before applying the adhesive, always spray with water.

3 For the dish, roughly break up the tiles with a hammer, and usin[g] mosaic nippers, cut into small, irregular pieces about 1–1.5cm (³⁄₈–⁵⁄₈in) in size (see also page 20 onwards). Place a larger pebble in the centre of the dish and four smaller ones around this. Then stick on the little fish and fill the remaining surface with pieces of tile. Place more tiles and little pebbles around the fish in the shape of a star (see photo). Then stick on the large fish and fill the remaining floor area almost to the edge with tiny pebbles. Keep working in a star shape. Cover the edge of the dish, first with the top stones, graduating to mini pebbles below. Ensure a good mix of large and small stones, as well as colour.

4 The flowerpot is only partially covered. Each of the four curves i[s] 15cm (6in) high – the shape can be drawn with a pencil. When laying, first make the borders top and bottom and then fill the area in between.

5 Leave to dry for at least 24 hours. Then spray the mosaic with water to prevent the flowerpot absorbing the moisture from the grouting compound too quickly. Grout and leave to dry thoroughly before cleaning.

# MARITIME MOTIFS

## Tips & Tricks

◆ When forming the background area of the dish, first lay the outer edging stones. This will give a clean edge. The edging stones should never hang over the edge of the dish.

◆ For areas that cannot be laid straight away, always wipe the excess adhesive away before it sets.

◆ To work on the spheres, place them securely on a round, card roll or a suitable round dish or pan with a smaller diameter.

### LEVEL OF DIFFICULTY
◎◎

### MOTIF SIZES

Dish approx. 25cm (10in) wide

Spheres approx. 8cm (3⅛in), 11cm (4¼in) and 14cm (5½in) in diameter

### MATERIALS

◆ Flexible tile adhesive or dispersion adhesive in white
◆ Grouting compound in white
◆ Adhesive primer

### DISH

◆ Flat dish in china or fine stoneware, 25cm (10in) wide
◆ Stoneware tesserae: approx. 100 x white, 60 x shades of blue and 1 x black, 2cm (¾in) square
◆ 20 iridescent glass tesserae in mother-of-pearl, 2cm (¾in) square

### DECORATIVE SPHERES

◆ Spheres in ceramic or Styropor®, 8cm (3⅛in), 11cm (4¼in) and 14cm (5½in) in diameter
◆ Stoneware tesserae in approx. 100 x white, 50 x shades of blue and 1 x black, 2cm (¾in) square
◆ 30 iridescent glass tesserae in mother-of-pearl, 2cm (¾in) square

### TEMPLATE
Page 130

## Dish

1 The dish is made using the direct method. Cut out a supply of stoneware and glass tesserae. For the spiral, you will need mainly conical stones (see page 26). The outside of the circle is laid with square-shaped stones; cut the stones into quarters with the glass nibbling pincers or a glass cutter (for stoneware mosaic) (see page 24 and 26). For the marine creatures, cut the stones according to the photo and the template; you will need to cut out round stones for the eyes (see page 27).

2 As described in the step-by-step instructions (see page 32), first lay the maritime creatures and surround these with small, irregular stones. Then lay the spiral, with a round-cut stone forming the centre, which should have a 1cm (³⁄₈in) diameter.

3 Continue by creating the edge to the circular centre area, as well as the outer edge of the dish, and then fill the free areas in between.

4 Leave to dry for at least a day and then grout and clean.

## Decorative spheres

1 Paint the spheres with adhesive primer and leave to dry. Then transfer the motifs with carbon paper.

2 Cut up a supply of tesserae using the glass nibbling pincers (not for use with stoneware tesserae!), the glass cutter or mosaic nipper for the fish and starfish according to the template and the photo (see page 20 onwards). Use irregular, angular shapes to fill in the background areas.

3 The fish and starfish are laid first, by applying the adhesive very carefully. The spheres are directly covered with the stones (see page 51). To achieve a flat surface, keep carefully pressing the tesserae flat using the palm of your hand. Start by covering half the sphere and leave to dry for 24 hours. Then turn and lay the other half.

4 Leave to dry for at least a day and then grout and clean.

# LANTERNS

## Tips & Tricks

◆ Clean your tools immediately with an old cloth, as dried-on silicone adhesive is difficult to remove.

◆ Have plenty of old cloths or kitchen paper to hand for cleaning and place the silicone paper underneath when laying, as the adhesive compound will always run a little. Only use the adhesive in a well-ventilated area, as the fumes could be harmful to your health.

◆ If your broken glass should contain the edge section of a car windscreen, use this for edging pieces (top and bottom), to reduce the risk of injury.

### LEVEL OF DIFFICULTY
↻

### MOTIF HEIGHTS
Glasses approx. 10cm (4in)

Dish approx. 15cm (6in)

### MATERIALS

◆ Glass dish, 15cm (6in), and various drinking glasses, 10cm (4in) high (flat surface)

◆ Grouting compound in white

◆ Broken glass from car windscreens

◆ Glass nuggets in various colours and sizes

◆ Silicone adhesive

◆ Alcohol or window cleaner and cloths

1 Clean the glasses thoroughly and rub them over with alcohol or window cleaner before covering to remove grease. The glasses must be dry before covering.

2 The pieces of broken glass are available in fairly irregular shapes. The individual fragments stick together in little groups. Try not to take these apart into individual pieces, only where you need to, so that you can follow the curve of the glass. The light refraction is prettier on pieces that have remained together. Use the small pieces just for filling the gaps. Glue the nuggets with their flat side to the glass.

3 Apply the silicone adhesive from the gun and spread using the modeller's spatula about 1mm ($\frac{1}{32}$in) thick. Only apply to an area that you can cover within five minutes. The glasses and dish are covered using the direct method (see page 48 onwards; step-by-step instructions on page 51). Start at the top edge. Where possible, avoid pointed pieces and leave space for a bevelled edge by gluing the glass pieces about 3–5mm ($\frac{1}{8}$–$\frac{3}{16}$in) away from the edge.

4 Leave the adhesive to dry for 24 hours, then grout the lanterns and finally clean thoroughly. To make the bevelled edge, apply the grouting compound at an angle from the top pieces of glass to the edge of the glass.

# ROSE SPHERES

Paint the spheres with adhesive primer and leave to dry. Paint the wooden rods to match the spheres and leave to dry. Then hold against the Styropor® sphere and draw on the diameter. Using a cutter or a pointed knife, cut a hole the right size and depth so that the rod can be inserted into it later.

Cut up the mosaic pieces. You will need conical pieces for the upper and lower areas of the sphere (see page 26) and squares for the rest (where necessary, cut into shape when working). When cutting, use smalti pincers, or glass nibbling pincers or a glass cutter, depending on the material (see page 20 onwards).

Mix the tile adhesive with colour pigment and water to make a soft compound, making sure to mix only a small amount of colour pigment at a time until the desired shade is reached.

The spheres are covered directly with the tesserae (see page 48 onwards). When working with smalti, you will need a raised adhesive bed, that is, the adhesive is applied more thickly and the stones are just pressed into it.

Start from the edge of the hole you have cut. First use stones in a light shade and gradually move on to a darker shade, or work the other way around. Stick on some glass nuggets or beads around the middle of the sphere. Apply the adhesive in a layer about 3–4mm 1/8in) thick, but only apply to an area that you can cover within 10 minutes.

To achieve a flat surface, keep carefully pressing the tesserae flat with the palm of your hand. Only cover half of the sphere first of all and leave to dry for 24 hours. Then turn and lay the other half. Finally, stick onto the rod.

## LEVEL OF DIFFICULTY
⟳

## MOTIF SIZE
Approx. diameter 12–15cm (4¾–6in)

## MATERIALS
- Styropor® spheres, 8cm (3⅛in), 10cm (4in) and 12cm (4¾in) in diameter
- 3 wooden rods, 1cm (⅜in), and 50cm (19¾in) in diameter, 60cm (23¾in) and 70cm (27½in) long
- Wood stain or acrylic paint in blue, green or red
- Smalti or glass tesserae: 30 x pink, 27 x lilac, 54 x violet, 50 x transparent red and 25 x transparent violet, 1cm (⅜in) square (pink/lilac-coloured sphere)
- Smalti or glass tesserae: 40 each x transparent light blue and sky blue, 50 x mid-blue and 15 x white, 1cm (⅜in) square, plus 11 beads in blue, 5mm (³⁄₁₆in) diameter (blue sphere)
- Smalti or glass tesserae: 35 x yellow and 26 x transparent yellow, plus 134 x shades of green, 1cm (⅜in) square (green sphere)
- Cement-based tile adhesive in white
- Colour pigment in blue, green or red

## Tips & Tricks

◆ When you are working on the sphere, place it on a glass or in a small dish with a smaller diameter.

◆ When working with glass tesserae, you can also lay the stones as described on page 48 onwards and grout. This will give a neat, even appearance.

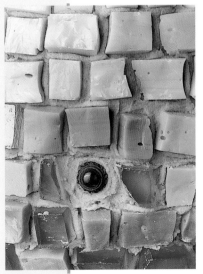

# WALL DECORATION

## Tips & Tricks

◆ Laying the circular area around the water pipe is easier if you draw on circles about 1.2cm (½in) apart.

◆ For the water pipe, a bamboo rod cut at an angle or a decorative tap would look good. You need to know before completing the mosaic how large the water pipe is. If necessary, make a slightly larger hole and fill it with silicone glue afterwards.

### LEVEL OF DIFFICULTY
◎◎◎

### MOTIF HEIGHT
Approx. 80cm (31½in)

### MATERIALS
◆ Styrodur® panel, 2cm (¾in) thick, 50 x 85cm (19¾ x 33½in)
◆ Approx. 400 glass tesserae in shades of green, 2cm (¾in) square
◆ Approx. 350 glass tesserae in shades of blue, 2cm (¾in) square
◆ Approx. 30 glass tesserae in shades of white, 2cm (¾in) square
◆ Approx. 20 glass tesserae in black, 2cm (¾in) square
◆ Approx. 300 glass tesserae in shades of brown and beige, 2cm (¾in) square
◆ Approx. 20 gold tesserae, 1cm (⅜in) (square)
◆ Mosaic glue or flour paste (see page 39)
◆ Cement-based tile adhesive in grey
◆ Grouting compound in grey
    ◆ Jigsaw with blade

### TEMPLATE
Page 130

1 Measure 55cm (21¾in) up from the lower edge of the Styrodur® panel. At this height, form a circle from the mid-point, drawing the curve of the semicircle 25cm (10in) radius as the top edge of the wall decoration. Saw out with the jigsaw.

2 Cut out the tesserae; for the circular area around the water pipe you will need conical pieces (see page 26). Most of the area around it can be filled with square shapes. Cut the tesserae into quarters using glass nibbling pincers or a glass cutter (apart from the gold tesserae, as they are already the right size) (see pages 24 and 26).

3 Then stick the picture with mosaic glue onto the paper design using the indirect method (see page 38 onwards). Lay the circles from the outside in, so that the outside circle ends in a full row of stones. Use longer pieces around the edge area (see small photo below left), rather than laying tiny stones next to one another. Leave to dry and cut off the excess paper with the cutter.

4 Mix the grouting compound so that it is free of lumps and not too runny. Mix the adhesive so that it is soft and free of lumps.

5 Paint the panel with an even layer of tile adhesive about 1–2mm (1/16in) thick.

6 Place the mosaic laid on paper onto a mobile base and grout from the reverse (see the step-by-step instructions on pages 40–41). Lay the panel covered with adhesive onto the reverse-grouted mosaic. Press together well, turn over and pack down with a trowel. Turning this large mosaic requires two people.

7 Wet the paper with hot water, allow to take effect and carefully peel back.

8 Clean the surface of the mosaic with a sponge and a little water. Pack down with a trowel and leave to dry.

9 Grout the whole surface again from the front and finally clean.

# PLANT POT WITH LIZARD

## Tips & Tricks

◆ The reverse of the plant pot is covered with pebbles and white stoneware mosaic (see small photo below).

◆ A table top can also be created using the lizard motif. Fill the area around it with white and red pieces as for the table with fish at the bottom of page 46. You can lay the edging using uncut tesserae as for the sun on page 122, and also alternating red and white (under every white stone around the edge of the table lay a red one and vice versa).

### LEVEL OF DIFFICULTY
◔◔

### MOTIF HEIGHT
Approx. 18cm (7in)

### MATERIALS

◆ Bulbous plant pot in white ceramic, 22cm (8¾in) diameter, 18cm (7in) high

◆ Approx. 300 stoneware tesserae in white, 2.3cm (¹⁵⁄₁₆in) square

◆ Approx. 30 stoneware tesserae in black, 2.3cm (¹⁵⁄₁₆in) square

◆ Small pebbles in various colours and sizes

### TEMPLATE
Page 129

1 Paint the base with adhesive primer and leave to dry. Transfer the outline of the lizard onto the plant pot using carbon paper.

2 Cut the black tesserae according to the template and picture using a glass cutter or mosaic nippers (see page 20 onwards). Cut the white tesserae into irregular pieces.

3 The plant pot is covered with tesserae using the direct method (see page 48 onwards; step-by-step instructions on page 51). Apply the adhesive in a layer about 1–2mm (¹⁄₁₆in) thick. Only apply as much adhesive as you can cover within 10 minutes. If you want to take a break from gluing, remove the excess adhesive from the object again using a modeller's spatula.

4 When laying the lizard, the main motif, begin by laying the outer stones first, then fill in the body (see page 14). It is best to lay the white stoneware pieces between the toes at the same time as laying the toes.

5 Then fill the area between the lizard body and the pebble border.

6 Continue working around the lizard, working with small and large, irregular shapes. Make sure that the lower edge is straight.

7 Then leave to dry for 24 hours and afterwards grout with a large, round brush. Finally, clean.

# DECORATIVE HEARTS

## Tips & Tricks

◆ Shells and pebbles are not grouted; instead, the thick adhesive bed about 3mm (⅛ in) creates a raised grout, that is, when you push the shells into the adhesive, some of it rises up and so avoids the need for grout.

◆ The smaller the individual pieces of material you use, the easier it is to make curves with them.

### LEVEL OF DIFFICULTY
☻

### MOTIF HEIGHT
Approx. 11cm (4¼in)

### MATERIALS

◆ Flat hearts in concrete, ceramic or Styropor®, 11cm (4¼in) high

◆ Approx. 35 mirrored glass pieces, shells, glass fragments or stoneware tesserae, 2cm (¾in) square

◆ Tile adhesive in grey

◆ Grouting compound in grey

◆ Adhesive primer

◆ Knife or all-purpose cutter

1 Paint the objects with adhesive primer, unless they are made of concrete, and leave to dry. We have used hearts here that have a smooth finish. If using Styropor® shapes, before priming cut down through the middle using a sharp knife or all-purpose cutter.

2 Then, where necessary, cut the tesserae with the glass nibbling pincers (not for stoneware!), the glass cutter or mosaic nippers (see page 20 onwards). Fill shells with a mixture of tile adhesive and quartz sand (ratio 3:1), spread the mixture smoothly and leave to dry. This will prevent them from breaking and provide a larger area for the adhesive.

3 Apply the adhesive about 1–2mm (¹⁄₁₆in) thick. Only apply as much adhesive as you can cover within 10 minutes. For objects that are to remain ungrouted, like those made using shells and pebbles, apply the adhesive a little thicker (see also Tip, top left).

4 Cover the mosaic objects using the direct method (see page 48 onwards). To achieve a straight edge, start with the outer edging stones and work inwards towards the middle.

5 Allow 24 hours to dry and then grout (apart from the hearts made from shells and pebbles). Finally, clean.

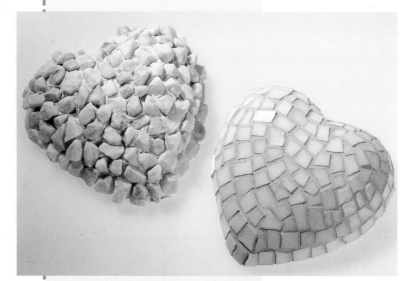

# MOSAIC ART

# PARROT

1 The parrot is laid using the indirect method (see page 38 onwards). First cut a supply of small glass stones for the bird using the glass nibbling pincers or the glass cutter (see pages 24 and 26). You will need mainly long shapes.

2 Then, using tesserae, lay the mirror image of the bird onto the drawing, working in the *Opus Vermiculatum* (see page 14). Start with the outer rows and work towards the centre.

3 Stick on the Greek Key borders using squares of the same size by cutting the stoneware tesserae into quarters. For stoneware, do not use the glass nibbling pincers; instead, use the glass cutter or the mosaic nippers. Where the pieces meet the bird, cut them exactly (see bottom Tip on the right). Stick on the background using whole stoneware pieces. Ensure that you make an exact cut where the background meets the motif.

4 Saw the pieces of wood exactly and stick to the MDF board using wood glue. Leave to dry. Then paint the MDF board with adhesive primer and leave to dry again. Attach the picture hooks to the back.

5 Grout the back of the reverse-laid mosaic and use the sandwich technique to put it on the board (see page 40, Step 6).

6 Then, as described in the step-by-step instructions on page 40, grout from the front and clean up.

## LEVEL OF DIFFICULTY
◔◔◔

## MOTIF HEIGHT
Approx. 60cm (23¾in)

## MATERIALS
- MDF board, 60cm (23¾in) square, 1.6cm (⅝in) thick
- Glass tesserae in shades of yellow, brown, green and red, plus black and grey, in total approx. 225 pieces
- Approx. 450 stoneware tesserae in white, 2.3cm (¹⁵⁄₁₆in) square
- Approx. 90 stoneware tesserae in black, 2.3cm (¹⁵⁄₁₆in) square
- Pieces of wood, 3cm x 5mm (1⅛ x ³⁄₁₆in), approx. 2.5m (2¾yd) long
- Wood glue
- Mosaic glue or flour paste (see page 39)
- Cement-based tile adhesive in grey
- Grouting compound in grey
- Adhesive primer
- Mitre saw
- Small nails
- 2 picture hooks, approx. 2cm (¾in) wide

## TEMPLATE
Page 128

## Tips & Tricks

◆ The parrot can also be included in a decorative wall scheme.

◆ You can varnish the wooden frame to match the motif. Paint before inserting the mosaic (Step 5).

◆ Where background stones meet the motif, draw the corresponding shape onto the stone to make cutting easier.

# FAMILY PICTURE

## Tips & Tricks

◆ You can attach picture hooks as shown in the small photo at the bottom of page 113; you will find another option for hanging the picture on page 116.

you will find another option for hanging the picture on page 116.

**LEVEL OF DIFFICULTY**
◶◶◶

**MOTIF HEIGHT**
Approx. 36.5cm (14½in)

**MATERIALS**

◆ Wooden board, 1.8cm (¾in) thick, 36.5 x 60cm (14½ x 23¾in)
◆ Plank of wood, 2cm (¾in) wide, approx. 2m (2¼yd) long
◆ 2 stoneware tiles with flower pattern, diameter 9cm (3½in)
◆ Stoneware tiles: 1 x dark red, 2 x orange patterned, 6 x ochre patterned and 10 x sky blue, 15cm (6in) square
◆ Stoneware tiles in reddish-orange with a star pattern, approx. 10cm (4in) square
◆ 1 tile each in pale yellow, yellowy-orange, lilac, rust brown, pale violet, white, dark green and dark grey, 10cm (4in) square
◆ Adhesive primer
◆ Acrylic paint in white
◆ 2 flat bars for hanging, approx. 2cm (¾in) wide
◆ Wood glue
◆ Grouting compound in beige
◆ Mitre saw
◆ Small nails
◆ Sandpaper

**TEMPLATE**
Page 129

1 Stick the planks of wood around the wooden board (see page 34); cut to fit using a mitre. Attach picture hooks (see Tip on the left). Sand the edges and corners, then paint the wooden board with adhesive primer and the frame with acrylic paint. Leave to dry and then transfer the template.

2 The mosaic is made using wood glue and the direct method (see the step-by-step instructions from page 32 onwards). Only apply the glue to the areas that you intend to work on straight away. Cut the pale yellow, yellowy-orange, pale violet, lilac, rust brown, dark green and red tiles into strips 1.5cm (⅝in) wide with the tile cutter (see pages 22 and 25).

3 Then nip the pale yellow and yellowy-orange tile strips with the mosaic nippers into 5mm (³⁄₁₆in) pieces and cut each strip into thirds to make 5mm (³⁄₁₆in) squares (see page 80). Lay the moon using the pale yellow squares and the sun using the yellowy-orange ones. Work from the outside in, giving the sun character.

4 Nip the pale violet, lilac and rust brown tile strips into 3mm (⅛in) wide strips. Stick on the face, glasses and nose using the pale violet and lilac strips, and use the rust brown ones for the hair.

5 Cut the red tile strips into 13 x 3mm (⅛in) wide strips and one 2cm (¾in) wide strip and the rest into irregular pieces. Stick the narrow mouths with the 3mm (⅛in) wide strips. Divide the 2cm (¾in) wide strip down the middle to make the two cherries and stick on. Use the remaining pieces to make the large mouth (for the child). Nip five 3mm (⅛in) wide dark green tiles for the stems of the cherries.

6 Cut two circles from the dark grey tiles (see page 27) and stick on as eyes. Cut about 12 small triangles from the white tiles and lay them around the grey ones for the whites of the eyes.

7 Break up the ochre patterned tiles with a hammer (see page 25) and cut the fragments into smaller pieces using the mosaic nippers. Select six small flowers from the fragments and cut into 1cm (⅜in) diameter circles, then lay as the noses and chests. Select the unpatterned fragments and use them to fill both the faces. Then nip about 30 long, thin strips and stick on to outline the chest. Fill the body with the remaining fragments (possibly even after laying the wings, see Step 8).

8 Break up the orange patterned tiles with a hammer and make the wings from the fragments. Break the two round tiles into three pieces each by striking with the hammer and stick on. Then nip out the pattern from the reddish-orange tiles with the nippers and stick on.

9 Break up the sky blue tiles and cut into small pieces. Use them to make the background together with some pale yellow, yellowy-orange and lilac pieces. Leave to dry overnight and then grout and clean.

# TURTLE

## Tips & Tricks

◆ The turtle can also be laid using the indirect method (see page 38 onwards), giving a nice, even surface that can be used for a table top, for example.

◆ To hang, drill holes into the back of the board and attach a flat bar over them.

**LEVEL OF DIFFICULTY**
☺☺☺

**MOTIF SIZE**
Approx. 66cm (26in)

**MATERIALS**

◆ Wooden board, 1.8cm (¾in) thick, 66cm (26in) square

◆ Plank of wood, 5mm (³⁄₁₆in) thick, 3.5cm (1³⁄₈in) wide, approx. 2.6m (3yd) long

◆ Stoneware tiles in 9 x various shades of brown, 5 each x four matt shades of gold, 1 x shimmering gold-tone, each 10cm (4in) square

◆ 18 stoneware borders in turquoise, 1cm (³⁄₈in) wide, 15cm (6in) long

◆ 25 stoneware tiles in various shades of dark blue to light blue, plus turquoise to water green (at least 15 different shades)

◆ 2 leftover pieces in dark grey (for the eyes)

◆ Cement-based tile adhesive in white

◆ Grouting compound in brown, turquoise and light grey

  ◆ Adhesive primer

  ◆ Sandpaper

  ◆ Mitre saw

**TEMPLATE**
Page 130

1 Cut the planks of wood to fit using a mitre and stick onto the wooden board using wood glue (see page 34; it is raised slightly in front and behind). Leave to dry. Paint the wooden board with adhesive primer and leave to dry again, then transfer the motif.

2 Cut the tiles in various shades of brown into irregular round, ova and organic shapes using the mosaic nippers (see page 27); in tota about 160 small pieces between 1–2cm (³⁄₈–¾in) in diameter are needed, as well as two somewhat larger shapes for the head. Cut th eyes from the dark grey leftover pieces.

3 Cut about 105 long, oval shapes appoximately 1.5 x 3cm (⅝ x 1⅛in) from the various gold shades to border the turtle's back. Cut various long pieces approximately 5mm x 1.2cm (³⁄₁₆ x ½in) from the remaining matt gold tiles to fill the turtle's shell. Cut about 15 1.5c (⅝in) diameter circles from the shimmering gold-tone tile.

4 Now lay the turtle using the direct method (see page 28 onward step-by-step instructions on pages 32–33). First lay the border to the shell, then fill the inner area. Afterwards, lay the flippers and head, also laying from the outside in (see also page 14).

5 When forming the background lines, follow the template and work with the flow of colours. Cut the tiles for the water backgroun with the tile cutter in 1.5cm (⅝in) wide strips. Break these strips using the mosaic nippers into 1–1.5cm (³⁄₈–⅝in) strips. Lay the wid strips using pale green shades and some dark blue. Divide the remaining pieces of tile again and use to fill the background area.

6 Leave to dry overnight. Then grout the turtle in brown. Leave to dry overnight again. Then grout the remaining background with turquoise and green grouting compound to match. Either keep leaving to dry as you go along or accept that the two grouting compounds will sometimes blend into each other, which can give a nice effect (see also page 19). Leave to dry overnight again and finally clean and polish.

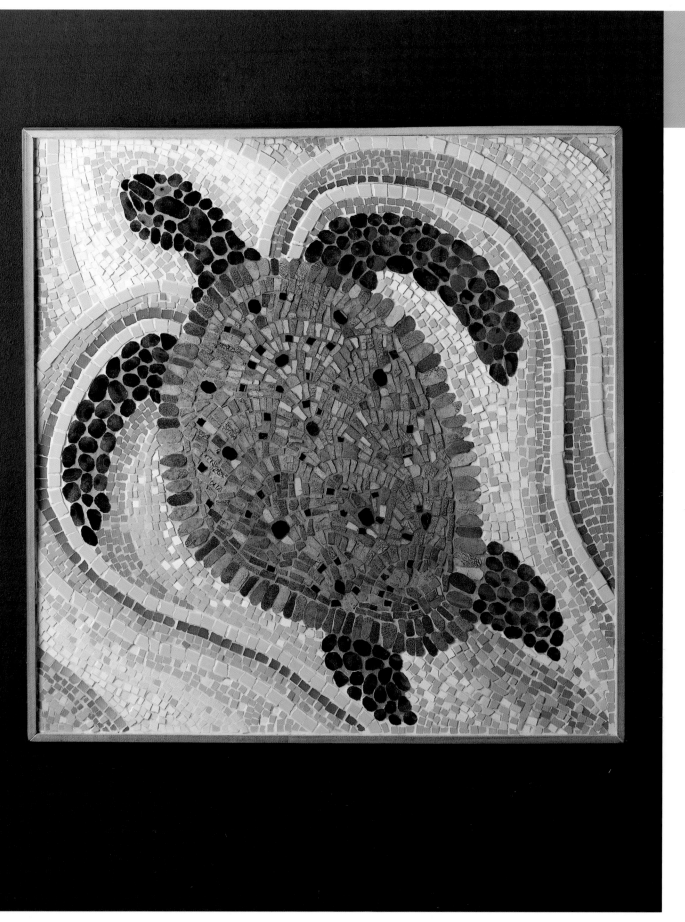

# TWO BIRDS

Saw the planks of wood to fit, stick to the MDF board with wood glue and also nail together. Leave to dry thoroughly. Then attach the picture hooks to the back.

Spread adhesive primer onto the MDF board and paint the frame with gloss. Leave to dry thoroughly again. Now transfer the design to the board using carbon paper.

Cut the smalti using smalti pincers or a hammer and awl (see pages 23 and 26), or simply use ready-made 1.7 x 1cm (¾ x ⅜in) smalti and only cut where you need to.

Apply the glue and cover the board using the direct method (see page 28 onwards; step-by-step instructions on pages 32–33). Only apply as much adhesive as you can cover within 10 minutes. The piece will be left ungrouted, which is why you need to use more glue, apply a layer about 3–4mm (⅛in) thick so that the adhesive rises into the gaps.

When laying the tesserae, work in the *Opus Vermiculatum* (see page 14), starting with the outlines of the birds.

Allow 24 hours for the mosaic to dry and then fill the edge area with trass cement/mortar or wall plaster and smooth the surface using a trowel and sponge (see page 45, Steps 10 and 12).

## LEVEL OF DIFFICULTY
◉◉

## MOTIF HEIGHT
Approx. 35cm (13¾in)

## MATERIALS
- MDF board, 1.6cm (⅝in) thick, 50 x 35cm (19¾ x 13¾in)
- Cement-based tile adhesive or dispersion adhesive
- Smalti in white, green, turquoise, brown and lilac, approx. 2.25kg (5lb)
- 10 gold tesserae, 1cm (⅜in) square
- Trass cement/mortar, grain size 0–4mm (0–5/32in) (for the background)
- Plank of wood, 3 x 1cm (1⅛ x ⅜in), approx. 1.8m (2yd) long
- Mitre saw
- Gloss paint in white
- Wood glue
- Adhesive primer
- Small nails

## TEMPLATE
Page 128

## Tips & Tricks

◆ As using a hammer and awl requires some practice, beginners would be advised to use smalti pincers for breaking up the material.

◆ Do not try to achieve a totally flat surface. Part of the attraction of the smalti lies in the different plays of light, which will change depending on the position of the stones.

◆ Once hardened, the trass cement/mortar surface can be easily coloured using diluted emulsion paint.

# FACES

## Tips & Tricks

◆ Carefully nip off the handles from the cups using mosaic nippers.

◆ Use tweezers to stick on the small beads.

◆ Make sure with bulbous pieces in particular that you apply enough adhesive. The individual pieces should sit fully in the adhesive.

◆ A 3cm (1⅛in) diameter metal washer can be stuck to the back of the frame using dispersion adhesive or flexible tile adhesive. When this has dried, drill a hole through the washer and use it to hang the picture.

**LEVEL OF DIFFICULTY**
◡◡

**MOTIF HEIGHTS**

China face approx. 25cm (10in)

Mask approx. 42cm (16½in)

**MATERIALS FOR THE CHINA FACE**

◆ Stoneware tiles as a base, 25 x 20cm (10 x 8in)

◆ Cement-based tile adhesive or dispersion adhesive in white

◆ Grouting compound in white

◆ Approx. 2 flat china or stoneware plates and large and small handles from cups

◆ Ceramic tiles in black, approx. 20cm (8in) square

◆ 2 each x conical shells, button mosaics and millefiori discs

◆ Pebbles, metal buttons, beads and glass nuggets

◆ Adhesive primer

**MASK**

◆ Hard foam board (Styrodur®), 1cm (⅜in) thick, diameters 30cm (12in) and 35cm (13¾in), and 2cm (¾in) thick, diameter 42cm (16½in)

◆ Old barrel hoop, diameter 42cm (16½in)

◆ 450 stoneware, glass and natural stone tesserae each in brown, red, beige and mustard, 1cm (⅜in) square

◆ Tiffany glass in green, white and brown, each 2.5 x 10cm (1 x 4in)

◆ 18 gold tesserae, 1cm (⅜in) square

◆ Cement-based tile adhesive in grey

◆ Grouting compound in grey

◆ Jigsaw and fine blade

**TEMPLATES**
Page 126

## China face

1 Prime the tiles and leave to dry. Roughly break the plates and ceramic tiles in a cotton or plastic bag (see page 25). Make the broken pieces of plate smaller using the glass cutter and breaking pincers or the mosaic nippers (see page 20 onwards). Make sure that you are wearing protective goggles.

2 Transfer the drawing to the stoneware tiles using carbon paper. Apply the adhesive about 1–2mm (1⁄16in) thick. Only apply as much adhesive as you can cover within 10 minutes.

3 Then lay the face. Start with outlining the eyes, insert the pupils and fill the area around with suitably cut mosaic pieces (see bottom Tip on page 113). Attach the handles for the nose and ears, the shells for the mouth and pebble for the chin. Then lay the rest of the face area using irregular pieces, working from the outside in; for the edge, use the factory-finished edge of the material where possible. Finally, lay the earrings. Leave to dry, then grout and clean.

## Mask

1 Bend the barrel hoop into an oval, transfer the shape onto the thick hard foam board and saw out using the jigsaw. Also saw out the small shapes and stick together in stepped layers using tile adhesive, then smooth over with the tile adhesive (see page 50).

2 Once it has dried, draw on the face and cover using the direct method. Start with the pupils (button mosaic) and work outwards. After the eyes, lay the black outline for the mouth and then the teeth and fill the background with red glass mosaic. Then lay the eyebrows and the dividing line from the lighter to the darker side of the face. Now lay the outer edge (continuous line) and then fill the face from the outside in.

3 Leave to dry for 24 hours and then grout.

# SUN

## Tips & Tricks

◆ Turning the board requires two people.

◆ In order to cut the stones to fit exactly, draw the shape onto them. They can be traced from the motif beforehand using tracing paper.

**LEVEL OF DIFFICULTY**
◌◌

**MOTIF HEIGHT**
Approx. 60cm (23¾in)

**MATERIALS**

◆ MDF board, 2.5cm (1in) thick, 60cm (23¾in) square

◆ Stoneware tesserae: 4 x black, 200 x white, 5 x green, 20 x apricot, 14 x beige, 100 x sand, 2 each x light green, grey and dark brown, plus 160 x terracotta, 2.3cm (15/16in) square

◆ Mosaic glue or flour paste (see page 39)

◆ Flexible, cement-based tile adhesive in grey

◆ Grouting compound in grey

◆ Adhesive primer

◆ Jigsaw with fine blade

   ◆ Sandpaper
   ◆ Large plastic sheet

**TEMPLATE**
Page 127

1 Saw a 59.3cm (23½in) diameter circle (from the MDF board using the jigsaw and attach the picture hooks to the back (see page 113). Then spread adhesive primer over the board, not forgetting the edge.

2 For the edge, keep the tesserae in their original size; cut almost all the other tesserae into quarters, as well as six terracotta pieces (reserve some stones in each colour for working on the face, as differently cut shapes will be needed for this). Use the glass cutter (preferably with a support board, see page 24) or mosaic nippers for cutting.

3 Stick the work onto the paper design using mosaic glue and the indirect method (see page 38 onwards; step-by-step instructions on pages 40–41). When you are laying the tesserae, start with the eyes, mouth, nose and chin, then fill in the face area. Next lay the edging stones as whole tesserae, then the sun's rays from quartered stones. Move on to lay the background area, working from the outside edge inwards using quartered stones. Always work in a circle until you reach the face area.

4 Leave to dry and cut off the excess paper with a cutter.

5 Stick the edging stones with tile adhesive to the edge of the MDF board (see page 34) and allow at least 24 hours to dry. To stick the edging stones, lay the MDF board exactly onto the laid mosaic; this requires two people, and stick the stones so that the gaps line up. For protection, lay a plastic sheet between the mosaic and the MDF board.

6 Mix the grouting compound so that it is free of lumps and not too runny. Mix the adhesive so that it is soft and free of lumps. Spread an even layer of adhesive over the MDF board about 1–2mm (1/16in) thick.

7 Place the paper-laid mosaic onto a mobile base (such as a wooden board and grout from the reverse. Lay the MDF board spread with adhesive onto the reverse-grouted mosaic. Press together, turn over and pack down with a trowel (see page 41). Also tap the edge with a trowel so that the horizontal stones butt up to the vertical ones (around the edge of the board); they must not overlap.

8 Once the grouting compound and adhesive have set, wet the paper with hot water, allow to take effect and carefully peel back. Clean the surface with a sponge and a little water.

9 Pack the surface down again using a trowel and leave to dry. Finally, grout the whole board again from the front and clean.

# THE MOON

## Advice

◆ The total surface of this moon is about 0.35m² (0.42yd²), so be sure to have enough materials ready!

### LEVEL OF DIFFICULTY
◔◔◔

### MOTIF HEIGHT
Approx. 60cm (23¾in)

### MATERIALS

◆ Papier-mâché moon, 30cm (12in) wide, 60cm (23¾in) long

◆ Glass nuggets in shades of yellow, 1.5cm (⅝in) diameter

◆ Transparent glass nuggets, 3–5mm (⅛–³⁄₁₆in) diameter

◆ Ceramic stars in yellowy-orange, 1.5cm (⅝in) diameter

◆ Millefiori discs in shades of yellow, 4mm (⁵⁄₃₂in) diameter

◆ Teddy bear eyes in yellow, 1cm (⅜in) diameter

◆ Glass tesserae in shades of yellow, 1cm (⅜in), 1.5cm (⅝in) and 2cm (¾in) square

◆ Some gold and silver tesserae, 2cm (¾in) square

◆ Ceramic tesserae in yellowy-orange, 2.5cm (1in) square

   ◆ Smalti in shades of yellow, 1 x 2cm (⅜ x ¾in)

   ◆ Various glass pieces in shades of yellow

   ◆ Mirror pieces in gold

   ◆ Acrylic paint in silver

   ◆ Transparent silicone adhesive

   ◆ Grouting compound in vanilla yellow

1 What the moon looks like depends very much upon the materials used – you will definitely need a large collection of materials. This piece is a good example of how you can combine found objects you may have with traditional glass and ceramic materials.

2 If you want to hang the moon up, then attach a loop to the top of the papier-mâché shape by puncturing two holes and threading a wire through.

3 Then paint the shape with silver acrylic paint, which will reflect the transparent materials better. When laying, work in the direct method (see page 51), starting with the eyes, then the mouth, nose, third eye and the remaining details. Where possible, draw on the pattern of lines from the diagram. Finally, fill in the background.

4 When creating the sculpture, be guided by the materials that you have available to you. The mysterious moon should appear friendly, impressive and inviting in this mosaic. This impression can be given by using gold, yellow and orange shades.

5 Finally, grout the moon and clean when dry.

# TEMPLATES

## Advice

◆ The templates have been reduced in size, but they can easily be enlarged to the size of the motifs featured in the Projects section using the suggested enlargement percentage or the grid. Follow the instructions, as well as the Expert Tip on page 13.

## Fish

Page 37

Enlarge template on 20mm (¾in) grid or by 400%

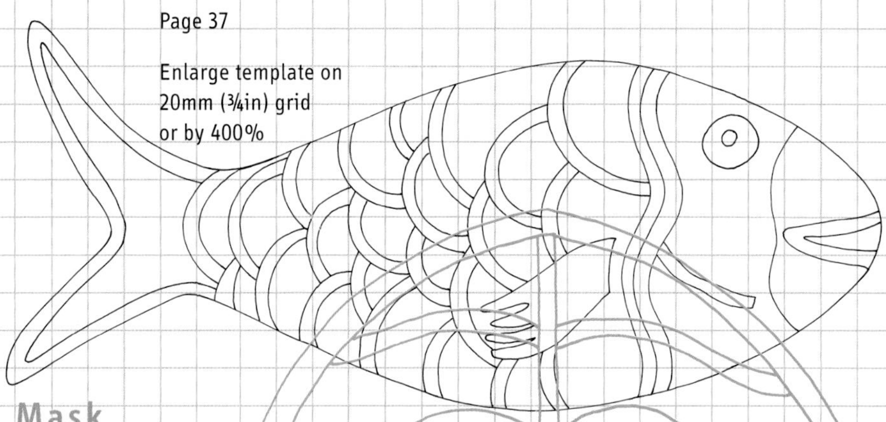

## Mask

Page 120

Enlarge template on 20mm (¾in) grid or by 400%

## China face

Page 121

Enlarge template on 20mm (¾in) grid or by 400%

## Bird

Page 47

Enlarge template on 15mm (⅝in) grid or by 300%

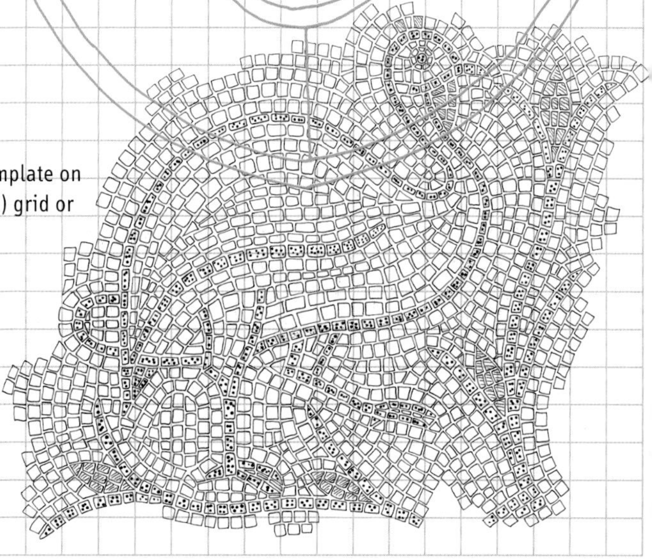

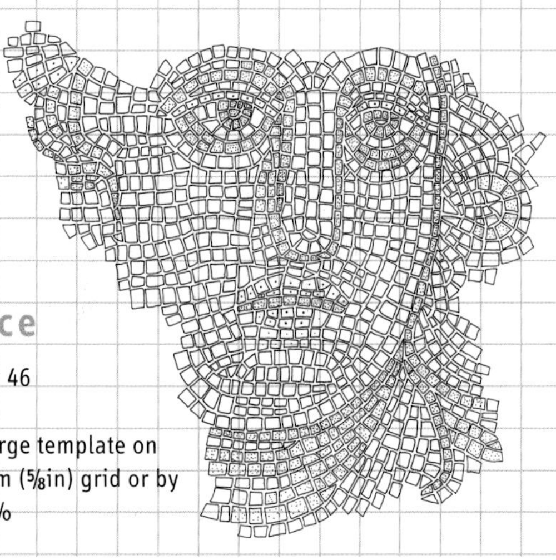

## Face

Page 46

Enlarge template on 15mm (⅝in) grid or by 300%

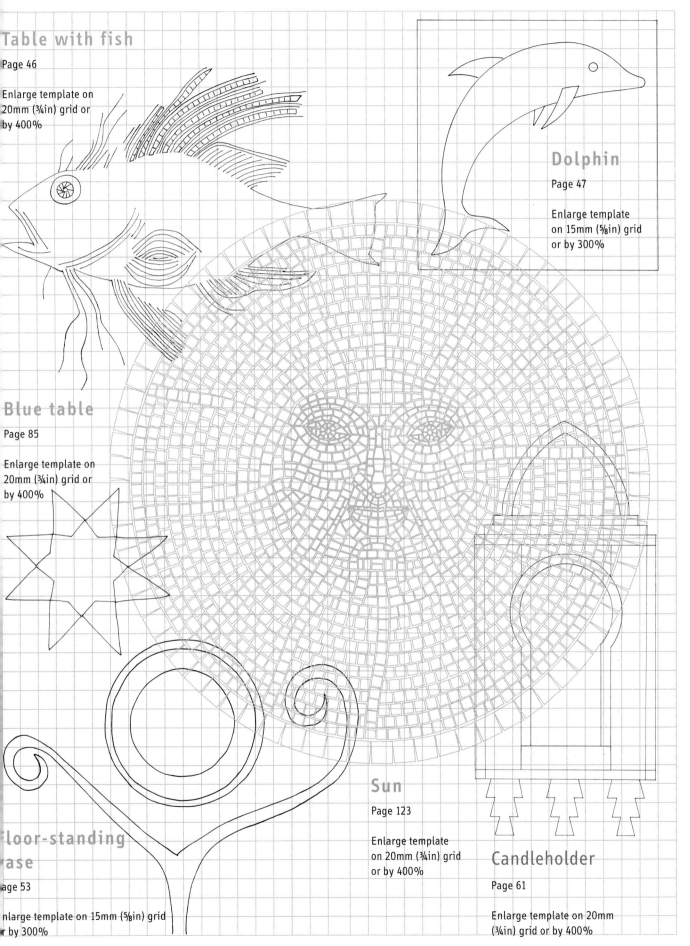

## Table with fish

Page 46

Enlarge template on 20mm (¾in) grid or by 400%

## Dolphin

Page 47

Enlarge template on 15mm (⅝in) grid or by 300%

## Blue table

Page 85

Enlarge template on 20mm (¾in) grid or by 400%

## Sun

Page 123

Enlarge template on 20mm (¾in) grid or by 400%

## Floor-standing vase

Page 53

Enlarge template on 15mm (⅝in) grid or by 300%

## Candleholder

Page 61

Enlarge template on 20mm (¾in) grid or by 400%

127

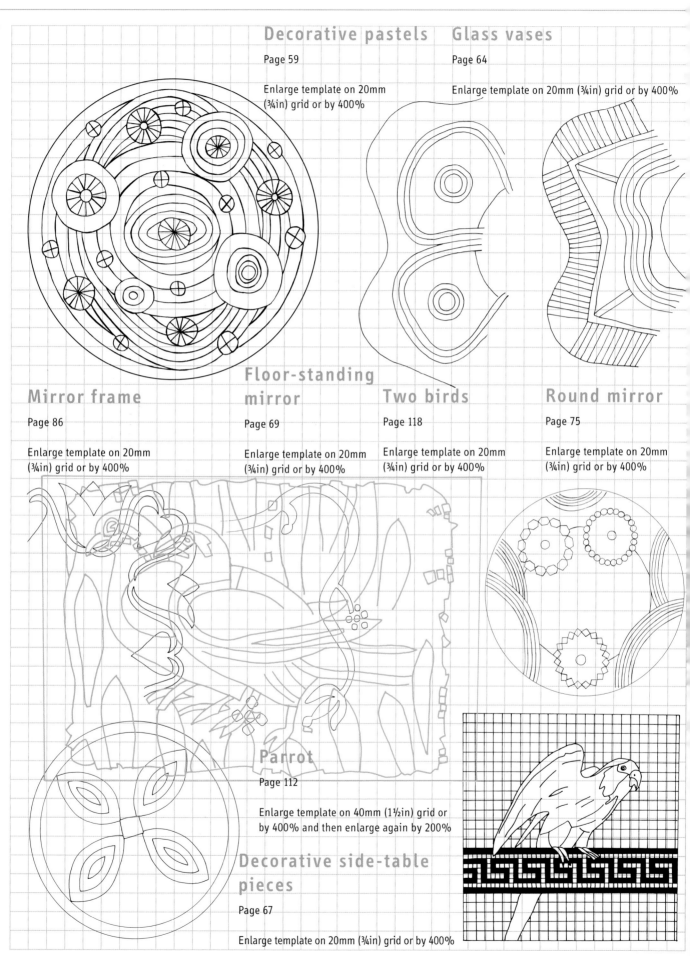

## Decorative pastels

Page 59

Enlarge template on 20mm (¾in) grid or by 400%

## Glass vases

Page 64

Enlarge template on 20mm (¾in) grid or by 400%

## Mirror frame

Page 86

Enlarge template on 20mm (¾in) grid or by 400%

## Floor-standing mirror

Page 69

Enlarge template on 20mm (¾in) grid or by 400%

## Two birds

Page 118

Enlarge template on 20mm (¾in) grid or by 400%

## Round mirror

Page 75

Enlarge template on 20mm (¾in) grid or by 400%

## Parrot

Page 112

Enlarge template on 40mm (1½in) grid or by 400% and then enlarge again by 200%

## Decorative side-table pieces

Page 67

Enlarge template on 20mm (¾in) grid or by 400%

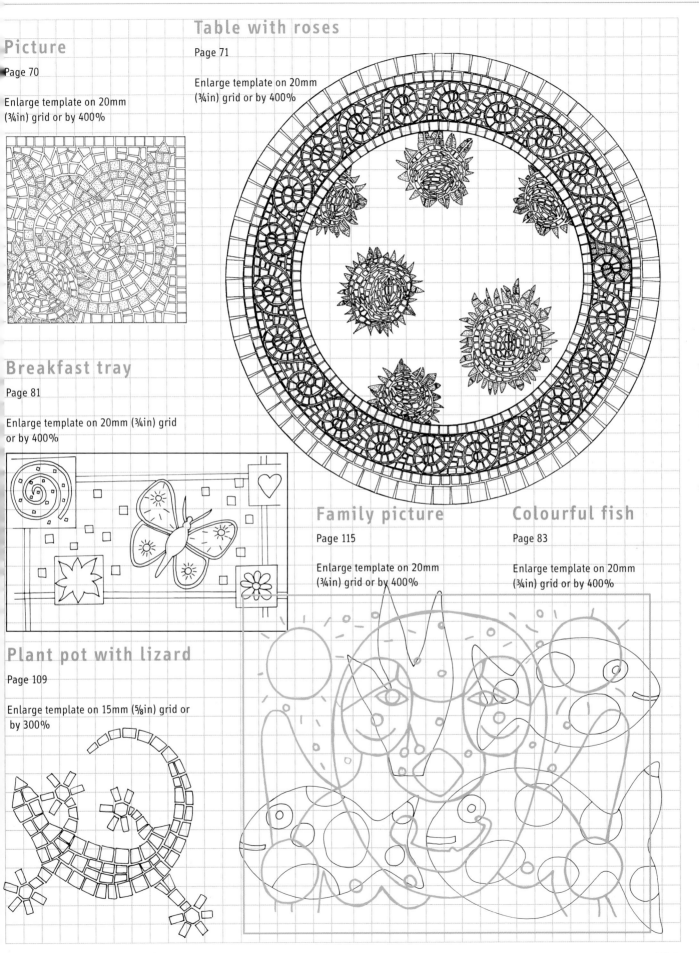

# Picture

Page 70

Enlarge template on 20mm (¾in) grid or by 400%

# Table with roses

Page 71

Enlarge template on 20mm (¾in) grid or by 400%

# Breakfast tray

Page 81

Enlarge template on 20mm (¾in) grid or by 400%

# Plant pot with lizard

Page 109

Enlarge template on 15mm (⅝in) grid or by 300%

# Family picture

Page 115

Enlarge template on 20mm (¾in) grid or by 400%

# Colourful fish

Page 83

Enlarge template on 20mm (¾in) grid or by 400%

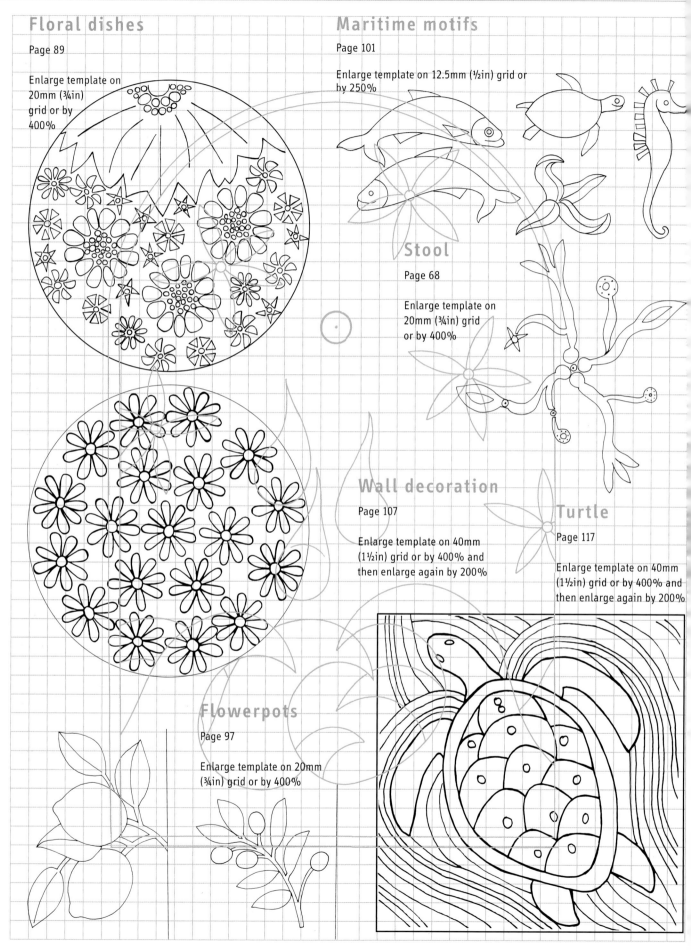

## Floral dishes
Page 89

Enlarge template on 20mm (¾in) grid or by 400%

## Maritime motifs
Page 101

Enlarge template on 12.5mm (½in) grid or by 250%

## Stool
Page 68

Enlarge template on 20mm (¾in) grid or by 400%

## Wall decoration
Page 107

Enlarge template on 40mm (1½in) grid or by 400% and then enlarge again by 200%

## Turtle
Page 117

Enlarge template on 40mm (1½in) grid or by 400% and then enlarge again by 200%

## Flowerpots
Page 97

Enlarge template on 20mm (¾in) grid or by 400%

# INDEX

Below you will find the most important terms used in the book in alphabetical order. The page number refers to the main entry in the book.

# AUTHORS

**Bruno Rodi** completed training as a mosaic artist from 1983 to 1985 at the Mayer'schen Hofkunstanstalt in Munich (Germany's leading glass mosaic and stained glass window institute). He then worked alongside international artists on mosaic projects in Munich, Hamburg, Vienna, Cairo and New York, and attended a further course at the Centro Internazionale Studi Insegnamento Mosaico in Ravenna, Italy. In 1989, he opened the Bruno Rodi mosaic workshop in Constance on Lake Constance and has since worked on commissioned pieces and provided project consultancy. Since 1995, he has offered a comprehensive range of courses for tile layers, teachers, artists and amateurs in the various techniques for designing mosaics. The experience he has gained from many years of teaching forms the basis of the Workshop section. For details of current courses and other information, please visit www.mosaikhandwerk.de.

**Catherine Massey** was born in France and moved to Hamburg 20 years ago. She has been involved with mosaics for ten years. She has her own studio and continually analyses materials and shapes that can be laid. She was trained in Paris and has run courses and workshops throughout Germany, as well as being involved in various projects, some with children. She has received commissions for decorative pieces right through to wall design and has been involved in exchange and collaboration with artists and artisans; all of which has formed her self-taught career. Her love of detail, together with the play between viewing up close and from afar, colours and materials, curiosity and friendship are all elements that guide her in her work. For details of current courses and other information, please visit www.galerie-galipette.de.

**Lea Ciambelli**, born in Naples in 1977, has been involved with mosaics since 1998. Her love of this art led her to Ravenna, via Florence, after leaving college. This is where she learned about the Byzantine mosaic technique at the Albe Stainer School of Mosaics. She went on to develop her knowledge at the 'Cooperativa Mosaicisti', one of the oldest mosaic workshops in the area. She then spent two years in Spain, where she made contact with 'La Red Arte Joven' association of artists, taking part in group and individual exhibitions. She ran mosaic courses and accepted private commissions. Now back in Italy for some years, she is involved in projects for making mosaics (such as a 250m²/299yd² floor mosaic in Luxembourg) and church apses in southern Italy and Boston, USA.